Comments j

This book really opened my e_ _ _ _ _ _ _ _ _ _ never know who had sex with whom, or who has STDs because we all look the same. Millions of accidental teenage pregnancies happen every year. So, as teenagers, we have to do our families a favor and focus on our books instead girls.

~Isaac N. Ekanem, 15

I'm not a big reader, but the title of this book and the sperm cells that look like balloons on the front just seemed interesting. For guys you hear, "wrap it up" more than you hear, "don't do it." The author realizes this and really makes a lot of good points. And it's not even boring. This book is good stuff.

~Darius J. Johnson, 22

As a guy who once left the church because of the pressure to practice abstinence until marriage, this book masterfully combines Biblical stories, science, and other real-life stories to make a very successful argument for young men to be abstinent until marriage. Kimberly presents the topic, not through scare tactics or through unrealistic statements, but as a caring mother who wants the best for her sons. There are even reflective questions that allow for real processing and honest thought from the reader. I can honestly say that if I had read this book 25-years ago, many of the decisions I made then would have been different. I am so excited about the impact this book will have on those who choose to read it. Two thumbs up!

~Napoleon A. Bradford, 39

DEDICATION

This book is dedicated to my sons, Zachary and Nicholas.

There are things our sons need to know about life that sometimes we, as parents, don't properly express. We just can't gather the necessary brain power to explain certain realities of life in the way our kids need it explained. This book is intended to fill the gap between what we share in the moment and that which we don't say.

CONTENTS

ACKNOWLEDGMENTS

I would like to acknowledge my husband, Troy G. Massey for being my number one supporter.

Condoms are cheaper than
child support and
abstinence is free.
Pay attention.

Unknown

1 ~ ABSTINENCE...NOT JUST FOR GIRLS

A book about abstinence, that's geared towards guys? It is the author's assumption that you did not purchase this book for yourself. Someone who loves you very much, and wants the best for you probably purchased this book in your honor, and hopes that you will not only read it, but take its contents to heart. Through your skepticism, you have read the first three sentences, and you are impressed. So far, the author doesn't expect you to read the book with great delight, but you still fear that this book will brainwash you, convert you—cause you to lose the bet you made with your friends. You know the bet, the dare, the competition as to which of you would lose your virginity first... This book goes against all of that, not to mention your own secret desires that you consider to be the "doorway to manhood." Keep reading, there are some things you may not have thought about just yet, and it is need-to-know information.

Reading this book will not brainwash you. After you read it, you will still be able to act on your own free-will, but your free-will will be more informed—more like that of a man.

Let's get started. Most states offer some form of health education course during which they explain the anatomy and physiology of the male and female reproductive systems. For guys, they explain the secondary sexual characteristics such as body hair and the deepening of the voice; they validate wet dreams, and they explain that the size of a man's penis is unrelated to his ability to father a child. In some states, you may have learned the proper way to put on a condom, using a banana as a prop. This book will not deal so much with the primary anatomical aspects of the reproductive system, rather the psychological and sociological aspects of sexuality, equipping you for good decision-making in regards to your sexuality, stressing the importance of good judgment and self-control.

First we must acknowledge the double-standard that exists regarding what males and females are taught about their sexuality. Girls are taught resistance and guys are taught moderation. Girls are taught to wait until marriage and guys are taught to try the milk before buying the cow. Girls are taught that having multiple partners makes them a slut, but guys are taught to sow their oats. It takes two. To teach girls to say no, but teach guys how to break down their resistance through lying and saying what they want to hear defeats the purpose of the abstinence lesson. Abstinence is not just for girls. Sexually transmitted diseases affect both genders. Guys can spread disease, just like girls can spread disease. When unexpected babies are conceived, both the guy and the girl experience major emotional turmoil. All of their plans and goals are disrupted, the relationship between them and their parents changes, they are forced to become adults when they would much rather remain in their youth. Guys need to be equipped with the mental and emotional presence of mind, to say no to sex, just as much as girls do. The consequences of poor sexual decisions are just as bad for guys as they are for girls. Good judgment and self-control are the keys to healthy relationships.

Think About It:

1-1 Why have you decided to read this book?

1-2 What do you already know about abstinence?

1-3 Have you noticed the double-standard the author wrote about? Do you believe this double-standard should continue to exist?

Right is right, even if everyone is against it, and wrong is wrong even if everyone is for it.

William Penn

2 ~ Okay...I Get the Point

"Take a beaker," was what Dr. Velini said to each of us as we entered the auditorium on the first day of Anatomy & Physiology, also known as BIOSC 235. Most professors started lecturing on the first day after they got all the logistics out of the way, but this guy...it seemed like he was about to make us do some kind of ice-breaker or something. He had a tray of small beakers sitting near each of the entrance doors to Smith Auditorium. Each beaker was about half full with what appeared to be water. I had taken several classes in Smith Auditorium, and I knew just where to sit. I had a spot with plenty of space for my long legs, a good view of all the girls as they entered, and it was at an angle off to the left. If I dozed or put an earbud in my ear, I would be safe. I sat back in my favorite seat, looking lanky, glancing around to see which of my female classmates would become my *study partner* for this class. I held my beaker of water, with my elbow on the armrest, as the room filled with people.

Pretty soon, Dr. Velini, a short, dark-haired guy from India, began to speak. His voice, amplified by the mic attached to his collar, "May I have your attention! May I have your attention!" The muffled sounds died down quickly. I am Dr. Paul Velini, I will be your Anatomy & Physiology instructor this semester." He told us where he graduated from and what he studied, and gave a little background as to what brought him to BNU. In his accent, he told us to get up and mingle with each other. "And as you mingle, I want you to share some of the water in your beaker. Pour some of your water into their beaker, then allow them to pour some back into your beaker. Does everyone understand?" It sounded simple enough to me. I had my eye on a couple of girls I wanted to mingle with anyway, so being told to do it, made thinking up a line unnecessary.

We all stood up and started looking around. There were at least 100 students in the auditorium. A dude sitting on the row behind me, said, "Hey, Man…" and he held out his hand to shake my hand, I shook his hand, but somehow trading water with him, just didn't appeal. I shook his hand, then immediately found this girl to start a brief conversation with and trade water. It didn't take long before I had exchanged water with…I don't know…nine or ten girls. And I got some numbers! Even better!

"Okay, please make your way back to your seats. Thank you. Thank you." Dr. Velini sounded over the speakers. Okay! Uh…" His accent seemed heavier now, "Okay, did you get to know some people? Did you get to exchange water samples? Guys, did you get some numbers?" He laughed. "Well, you all know that as a PhD, I have access to all sorts of chemicals and scientific supplies, well, let's suppose that your beaker of water isn't really water, let's suppose it's a mixture of your body fluids. What are body fluids?"

People started answering him aloud, "Urine!" "Blood!" "Saliva!" "Tears!" And someone from the back yelled, "Sweat!"

He waited, as if there was something else he wanted to hear, "Semen? Semen, nobody said that! What about vaginal secretions! Nobody said that either! Let's add those to the list. Well, suppose you have a container of your body fluids, and you just exchanged them with somebody else. What are some ways body fluids can be exchanged?"

I sat quietly, but many of my classmates were now a bit looser and didn't mind yelling out responses that were taboo. "Having sex!" "Kissing!" "Sneezing!" "Sharing towels!" "On workout equipment!" "Drinking after people!"

"Yes, you are all correct! Body fluids can be exchanged in many different ways. Sometimes it's intentional, but there are times when body fluids are exchanged unintentionally...right? Well, whether you mean to do it or not, when you exchange body fluids with somebody, you run the risk of being infected by any viruses or bacteria they may be carrying. All of you have seen strep throat go through an entire household, or mono cause a football team to forfeit the season because the players were too sick to take the field. Well, here on your first day of Anatomy & Physiology, as you begin this fall term, I want to make you aware of some things as they pertain to sharing body fluids." His accent was killing me!

He continued, "First of all, is there anyone in the room, who did not share their body fluids during the mingle time?" He looked around, no hands were raised. "So, with the mere suggestion that you exchange fluids, you all did it? I suspect that with the mere wave of bye-bye from your parents, that

11

freedom-factor kicked in and many of you will start sharing your body fluids with people you meet here at BNU. Did you ask any questions of the person you shared your water with here today? Did you at least find out how many people they had shared with previously? Because, you know…when you share fluids with someone, you're also sharing with the people they've shared with before you came along. And body fluids…they all usually look alike, those little viruses like HIV and Herpes Simplex, and bacteria like Syphilis and Gonorrhea, and Chlamydia, you can't see them. It might be there, but you can't see it. And it's very present among young people—especially college students. People who engage in casual sex have even more of these bugs. Casual sex refers to sex without commitment…multiple sexual partners." Dr. Velini was talking too much on this first day of class.

"Okay, so now that you've exchanged with three, four…nine different people, you just might start to become hypersensitive, paying attention to every little itch or discoloration. You might decide that maybe, just maybe, you should get checked. So, now it's off to the doctor." His teaching assistants were waiting with eye-droppers to walk around and test everyone's *body fluids.*

The first girl up at the front of the room was a real pale, anorexic-looking, red-head with freckles. She stood as she was asked, and faced the room. Dr. Velini tested her beaker and it turned hot pink. Her eyes got big as she looked nervously at everyone staring at her. My heart sunk! I had exchanged with her out of pity because she looked like no one was talking to her. Dang! Quickly, Dr. Velini and his team made their way through the room with testing droplets. Some people tested negative, but there was a convincing number of people now holding hot pink beakers of…sickness. There was

12

loud whispering and people were looking around desperately. I tested positive! I knew it! Man! It was that girl up at the front! I was looking around at what seemed like sixty-percent of the room now holding positive beakers, and I was so embarrassed. It was like I had wet my pants or something. This wasn't supposed to happen to me. I was clean-shaven, smelled good, always wore business casual, even to class...and now I've got...that *burn!* I wasn't the only one, but I felt like it. I always felt like I could basically do whatever I wanted without too much consequence, but this...this was pretty bad—it carried weight. If I was positive, how would that affect how people viewed me? I tried to avoid the eyes of the other people I traded with, figuring they wouldn't be chasing me down after class to get my number or friending me on InstaPost. This was not something that needed to happen on the first day of class. I felt like walking out right then, heading over to Young Hall to change my schedule, maybe even my major, because...

Once everyone had been tested, Dr. Velini started talking again, "Okay, so I guess it's pretty apparent that many of you tested positive for the infection of the hour...and many of you have been distraught with questions, and you're attempting to retrace your steps. Well, this simulation is so much like real-life, I can hardly stand it!" He laughed. And he was the only one laughing. "Not only are you getting a little sexuality lesson today, but you're also learning the basics of epidemiology." He laughed again, "I see the concern on many of your faces. I saw the fear in your eyes as you held out your beaker for testing. I saw you sink within yourself as you tested positive, and...I saw the nonchalance with which you were initially exchanging body fluids. If you take nothing else with you today, please take with you the lesson in how quickly a bacterium or virus can spread from person-to-person

13

contact. You have got to be mindful of this as you conduct your lives as young college students. You cannot make assumptions about other people. You have got to ask questions. You have got to take the time to get to know each other before you engage in sexual intercourse. You cannot ignore their sexual history—it does affect you. What's in the past does not always remain in the past, sometimes it rears its ugly head. There's a term many of you heard long ago, you may not have heard it in a while, you may have even forgotten how to spell it. The word, my friends, is abstinence. Abstinence means to do without, to withhold, to desist, to say no, to decline participation. And it works! If you choose to abstain from sexual relations, you will not have to wonder if you been tagged by Syphilis, pinned by Gonorrhea, or shot by HIV. You will be free of fear, worry, and concern. Abstinence, try it, it works!" He paused as he scanned the room.

I heard everything he said, and truly, it was making me think. Think I might need to get tested for real, because, there had been some careless moments, although I felt fine. And I was angry, angry that that girl up at the front had infected me.

Dr. Velini continued, "Now, about those body fluids...one of you picked up my beaker of sodium hydroxide, the rest of you had water. Everyone, please look down into your beaker and see if you have a small blue dot on the bottom of your beaker."

Low and behold, holy crap! I thought I was going to die. It was me. I had the beaker with the blue dot. I was the one who started all of this. I had the beaker with sodium hydroxide, everybody else in the room had water. That girl, didn't give it to me—I gave it to her...OMG! But, there was no way in the world I was going to raise my hand and admit it. I started looking around for the culprit just like everyone else was doing. "Okay," Dr. Velini spoke again, "Boy, this simulation continues to mimic real life...even with the simulated body fluids, the originating person has exercised his right to privacy." He laughed. "I know which of you it is, but I promise not to hold this against you when I grade your first test." Everybody laughed. I hoped he would just keep talking and dismiss us...fast. I got the point.

Think About It:

2-1 How does the sharing of body fluids spread infectious disease?

2-2 In what ways can a sexual partner's past experience(s) be dangerous to a current or future partner?

2-3 Why is it important for couples to have open and honest conversation before engaging in sexual activities?

2-4 How does abstinence work to prevent the spread of disease?

2-5 If you infected someone with a disease would you admit it?

2-6 Did <u>you</u> get the point?

If you can control yourself
sexually, you can control
yourself. Period.

A.C. Green

3 ~ Virginity

It was probably around eighth grade, age thirteen or fourteen when you first gave any thought to driving a car. You may have been asked to go outside and warm up the car on a cold morning, or your parents may have allowed you to drive around the cul-de-sac, or out on an old, deserted road. As time went on, your desire to become a legal, licensed driver grew. In high school, the desire was compounded as your friends showed off their licenses, and their parents bought them cars. By age sixteen, you couldn't wait to get your license! It meant freedom; it meant maturity; it meant you could come and go as you pleased! You had to have it!

When you finally got your license, whenever it was, your parents probably sat you down and gave you the rules of the car. No talking on the phone. No texting. No speeding. No loud music. No more than two friends in the car. No driving friends' cars. No staying out past 11pm. All of this freedom you thought you were about to have became a series of rules to keep you safe.

So, you're eighteen and you're a virgin, and you think that's way too old to still be a virgin. You think you should have lost your virginity the day after you got your driver's license! You think you should have lost your virginity at least two years ago. And you've been so close, but something has always interrupted the flow. You may still be a virgin, but it's certainly not due to the lack of trying. It is okay!

The virgin stigma is in your mind. There is no age at which a person is too old to be a virgin. Virginity should last until marriage. A. C. Green, an NBA star, was a virgin until he was 38 years-old and married. He is quoted as saying, "Kids are dying from causes of sexual activity. You're not going to find a tombstone stating that Frankie died because he was a virgin."[Webster]

Philip Rivers, the San Diego Chargers' quarterback was a virgin until he married. He believes chastity [abstinence] is a judge of character and shows a person's discipline. Ricardo Kaka Leite, a player on the Brazilian soccer team was a virgin until he married his wife, Caroline. He says that he thinks their life today is beautiful, "because we waited." [Top]

How is this for a pick-up line? "I just moved here from Arizona, and I'm trying to live right." Well, it worked! Prince Amukamara, cornerback for the Jacksonville Jaguars met the woman he eventually married at a nightclub and remained a virgin until they were married.[Boniello] Amukamara is also different from the norm because during a 2013 interview, he told reporters that he had never had a sip of alcohol in his life. Later he was asked, how he blew off steam without drinking and without sex. His response, "I still enjoy going out. I still enjoy dancing, and I get high off everyone else's high. If everyone is having a good time, that makes me have more fun, even though I don't need everyone to be happy for me to be happy, if that makes sense."[Staff]

There are some notable females who maintained their virginity until marriage, too. Singer, actress, and fashion designer Jessica Simpson was a virgin until she married at age 23. In an interview with MTV, she said, "I definitely think [abstinence] is the best birth control. I know that condoms are not a hundred percent, because I'm here because of a busted condom."[Simpson] She went on to explain that her birth was unplanned, and her mother confirmed. Virgins have no worries. They know they have no STDs, and they know their relationships are not about playing games. There is nothing wrong with being a virgin. Virginity is peace of mind.

Think about your friends who lost their virginity early on. Sex for them likely became a game, a numbers game—in more ways than one. On the one hand they were not satisfied having had sex with one girl, they wanted to accumulate a history by having sex with as many girls as possible. Anyone with a sexual history shares that sexual history with future sex partners because new partners are exposed to the potential STD's their partner's previous partners had. So, the more sexual partners a guy racks up, the more likely he is to contract an STD along the way—even if he uses a condom each time, the potential for exposure remains.

The numbers game becomes real serious when one of the girls calls and tells him that her period is late and he asks, "how many days late?" Eventually, if a person has sex enough times, a pregnancy will result—sometimes it happens after the first time, sometimes later, but it will happen. Eventually, if a person accumulates sexual partners who are also each accumulating other sexual partners, an STD will result. Which STD—it could be something that can be treated by five days on an antibiotic, or it could be a virus that has no cure at all and will lead to death.

As a virgin, you have none of those worries, none of those stressors. You don't have to play the virgin game with your friends. If they laugh at you, rest assured that you will get to laugh at them once the itching begins. Don't feel pressured to do what your friends do, be your own person, independent-minded, and confident that you do not have a baby on the way, and that you are not infected with an STD.

Think About It:
   3-1 Why do you think the virgin stigma exists?

   3-2 What do you think of A. C. Green's quote?

   3-3 Are you surprised at the number of professional
        athletes who practiced abstinence until marriage?
        Why are you surprised? Does their courage give you
        hope?

3-4 What do you think of Jessica Simpson's quote?

3-5 Virginity is peace. Explain that statement

Quote by A. C. Green from www.goodreads.com accessed June 11, 2011

Webster, A. G., Green, L. L., Green, R. S., Myra Wallace, Malik Yoba (Foreword), Karen Dick (Foreword), Edwin Louis Cole (Editor), A.C. Green (Foreword by), & (Foreword), J. J. (n.d.). A.C. Green. Retrieved June 11, 2011, from http://www.goodreads.com/author/show/794019.A_C_Green

Simpson, Jessica – Interviews, news, newspapers magazines, radio, TV, internet. (n.d.) Retrieved September 8, 2016

Top 9 Athletes Who Shockingly Waited/Are Waiting Until Marriage. (n.d.). Retrieved December 27, 2016, from http://www.thesportster.com/entertainment/top-9-athletes-who-waited-until-marriage/

Boniello, K. (2014, October 05). How Amukamara met and wooed his wife. Retrieved December 27, 2016, from http://nypost.com/2014/10/05/giants-cornerback-met-his-wife-at-nightclub-and-wooed-her/

Staff, B. (2013, September 17). Virgin NFL Player Says Teammates Call Him "The Black Tim Tebow" For Choosing Sobriety Over Slizzard Shenanigans With Groupie Slores. Retrieved December 27, 2016, from https://bossip.com/836006/

Self-control is the chief element in self-respect, and self-respect is the chief element in courage.

Thucydides

4 ~ In the Long Run

So, when should you lose your virginity? You should lose your virginity when you get married. Your honeymoon should be a very exciting event, anticipated by both you and your wife. It should mark the end of your single life, the end of your virginity, and the beginning of your happy marriage.

To maximize the excitement and anticipation you feel on your wedding night, you must employ self-control in your dealings with young ladies in high school and college. Developing this self-control now will even help you to maintain a faithful marriage. Rid your mind of the notion that marriage is the end of sexual temptation. Married men still have eyes and they are still surrounded by beautiful women. Married men may be wearing a wedding band on their finger, but that ring alone does not prevent women from flirting with them. A wedding ring also does not prevent married men from thinking they can pursue relationships outside their marriage. Married men continue to be tempted towards sexual relationships with former girlfriends, coworkers, the wives of their friends, etc. These relationships are often what destroy marriages.

About 57% of married men admit to having cheated at some point in their marriage.[Infidelity] Infidelity (cheating on one's spouse) is a major violation of the oath taken in the presence of friends and family—to live monogamously in marriage. The hurt and disappointment the wife feels when she finds out is sometimes irreversible and can lead to divorce. The trust and confidence that was once felt is replaced by disdain and doubt. About half of all marriages end in painful divorce.[National] This pain is not only felt by the deceived wife, but also by the guilty husband. Both of them had intentions of being married for life, they had built a life together, they might have children who will be hurt by the divorce. Their family and friends thought they were the perfect couple, but now they have property to divide. For her, being deceived by the one person in her life she thought would always be a constant confidant causes major grief. You can start preventing yourself from ever causing this type of pain to your wife and family by developing self-control right now.

To protect your future marriage, it is imperative that you learn to say no to sexual opportunities and walk away from sexual situations. The same self-control that you develop now will help you to walk away from unhealthy sexual advances in the future. They say you can't teach an old dog new tricks. The opposite would be that the best tricks are learned during youth. Start now, look at the world with a wider lens and see it for what it really is. Understand that casual sex carries risks that extend for an infinite period of time. The tricks to abstinence are the development of self-control and good judgment.

Think About It:

4-1 Do you plan to get married? How will the development of self-control now help you to maintain a healthy marriage?

4-2 Aside from making good sexual decisions, how will the development of self-control and good judgment help you in the long run?

Quote by Thucydides www.goodreads.com June 12, 2016

Infidelity Statistics. (n.d.). Retrieved June 17, 2011, from http://infidelityfacts.com/infidelity-statistics.html

National Marriage and Divorce Rate Trends. (2015). Retrieved December 18, 2016, from https://www.cdc.gov/nchs/nvss/marriage_divorce_tables.htm

Testosterone may be the underlying cause of sexual desire, but self-control and good judgment must be the rule.

A Guys' Guide to Abstinence

5 ~ TEST-O-STERILTY

At some point in your life, females began to look different in your eyes. Think back, remember when the females in your age group started to take on a more matronly figure with wider hips, a narrower waist, more full, rounded breasts? Remember when their voices lost their squeak? And as if those physical changes weren't enough to draw your attention, they started wearing makeup and perfume. The new era of the females in your age group caused a new level of intrigue in you, as well. As you observed the changes in their body, you began to ponder ideas about how your new manly body could intermingle with their new womanly body. Of course, your eyes have a lot to do with the ideas that develop in your mind. Your ideas also come from the images you see on TV, the lyrics you hear in music, and roles you see playing out with married couples in your life. Don't be alarmed, the ideas you had, and still have, are normal (for the most part). Those ideas, however, are not due only to your eyes. Testosterone, a chemical produced in your testes (the organs inside the scrotum) is largely responsible for this, and

28

it was only a matter of time.

Testosterone was the hormone, that, while still in your mother's womb, caused your testes to form and descend (in most boys) before you were born. Testosterone is the chemical that makes you male. As you reached puberty, your levels of testosterone increased tremendously, causing an increase in the growth of body hair, greater bone density, increased muscle mass, and thicker vocal cords, thus a deeper voice.[Effects] Additionally, you began to produce sperm cells—the male reproductive cell, by the billions! Those are not balloons on the front cover of this book. Those are sperm cells! About 1,500 sperm cells are produced each second! It is estimated that a single milliliter (1mL) of semen, contains 20,000,000 to 150,000,000 sperm cells.[How] Sperm cells are made in your body 24/7. You don't have to think about making them, and you can't stop them from being made. Not only does testosterone cause the mass production of sperm cells, it triggers the male brain to look for eligible recipients for those eager little cells. Quickly, you choose a female characteristic or two to focus on—her eyes, her breasts, her legs, her skin, her personality, her hands, her lips, something, to narrow the options, and you show off your attributes—your muscles, your deep voice, your athletic ability, your height, to entice her towards a union.

Everything mentioned above is natural. Puberty happens to everyone—everyone who is privileged to live that long, anyway. Sperm production is a natural, normal process that begins to occur as adolescent males enter manhood. Puberty in females brings about womanhood. Men and women are supposed to be attracted to each other. If they were not, reproduction would become slow, and the human race could become endangered, and if nothing changed, humans could become extinct. Imagine that! Not to worry, humans are far from extinct—the mechanisms of human attraction are working extremely well! Male-to-female attraction is BOOMING! Males are lying, cheating, and scheming to share their sperm cells with females. According to the CDC (Centers for Disease Control) about 10,926 babies are born in the United States every single day in recent years. That amounts to 3,988,076 babies born in a year. If you had trouble reading that number, it's three-million-nine-hundred-eighty-eight-thousand-seventy-six. [Births] With numbers like that we can rest-assured that sperm production is not on the decline.

Is testosterone really capable of affecting a person's brain? Something you may not know, is that females also produce testosterone—low levels of it. The hormone is produced and secreted by the female ovaries and adrenal glands. Women with testosterone levels that are lower than the norm tend to show little or no interest in sex. Men whose testosterone levels are less than 300ng/dL of blood (a condition commonly called Low T), also complain of low sex drive, erectile dysfunction, mood swings, fatigue, and trouble sleeping. [Low] Yes, testosterone, does affect the brain. While it does drive our desire to engage in sexual activities, we must employ good judgment and self-control so that we engage in healthy relationships.

The CDC, in addition to their report on the rising birth rate, reports that STDs (Sexually Transmitted Diseases) are also rampant—especially Syphilis, Gonorrhea, and

Chlamydia—with 19,000,000 new cases each year. That number, if you had trouble reading it, is nineteen-million. And the largest infected demographic is people between the ages of 15 and 24 years-old.[Sexually] The CDC estimates that nearly 50,000 people are infected with HIV (Human Immunodeficiency Virus) each year. This virus first appeared in 1981, and thirty-years later, there is still no cure, nor any acceptable vaccine. HIV infection leads to AIDS (Acquired Immune-Deficiency Syndrome) which currently leads to death—there is no cure. Testosterone may be the underlying cause of sexual desire, but self-control and good judgment must be the rule.

Think About It:

5-1 Can you list 5 things you learned about testosterone?

5-2 What statistic is also on the rise along with birth rates? How might these two be related?

How a Man Produces 1,500 Sperm a Second. (n.d.). Retrieved June 16, 2016, from http://news.nationalgeographic.com/news/2010/03/100318-men-sperm-1500-stem-cells-second-male-birth-control/

Births and Natality. (2016). Retrieved August 8, 2016, from http://www.cdc.gov/nchs/fastats/births.htm

Low Testosterone - WebMD: Symptoms, Health Effects, and Testosterone Replacement. (n.d.). Retrieved September, 2016, from http://men.webmd.com/features/low-testosterone-explained-how-do-you-know-when-levels-are-too-low

Sexually Transmitted Diseases in the United States, 2008. (n.d.). Retrieved September 18, 2010, from https://www.cdc.gov/std/stats08/trends.htm

Effects of Testosterone. (2014). Retrieved June 29, 2016, from http://www.healthline.com/health/low-testosterone/effects-on-body

A moral being is one who is capable of reflecting on his past actions and their motives – approving of some and disapproving of others.

Charles Darwin

6 ~ *H*is *I*nitial Venture

She hadn't been at my school for too long. Maybe I
had seen her second semester last year, I wasn't sure, but if I
had seen her I could've easily missed her. She always had on
dark colors, she wore her hair pulled over her eyes, and she
wore long sleeves even when it was hot outside. And she
never said a word...to anybody...like she was so quiet that
people didn't even try to figure her out. I mean, there's shy,
there's timid, and then there's Danique. When the teacher
called role, she didn't answer. Mrs. Littles had to look over
there to know she was present. Mrs. Littles was not shy either,
but she wouldn't call on Danique, like she thought it was too
painful or something to call on her and make her strain her
poor little unused larnyx or something. Danique wouldn't
even get in a group with anyone when we were allowed to
work with a group, she just sat there by herself with her head
down, eyes covered by her hair, and it frustrated me. I'm an
outgoing guy. I play football—running back, everybody
knows me, I got plenty of girls trying to get with me, but not
this one. She was sitting by me, but she might as well have
been sitting by the wall, 'cause I was nothing to her. The other
thing about me is I'm a code-cracker. I can't just leave a bad

situation as a bad situation. I can't leave a rock unturned. I can't stand to have a girl nearby whose eyes don't light up when I'm there. So, after about three or four weeks, I started trying to get Danique to talk...it was my mission.

We were in US History together, and there were too many kids for everybody to have a desk. The two of us had to sit at a counter on a couple of stools. When Mrs. Littles would pass papers down the row, they came to Danique, then she would have to hand me mine. Well, I started by bumping her arm when I reached for my papers, then, I would ask her like, "Did you hear what we're supposed to be doing?" and to that she always shook her head no. Then I started scooting my stool over closer to hers, so our arms were touching each other for the whole block. One day I told her my butt was hurting from sitting on the stool and I wanted to know if she would mind if I leaned on her because my butt was hurting. I finally got a response. She moved her hair out of her eyes and gave me the coldest look a girl can give a guy. Her eyes were NOT pretty. There was no glimmer. She wasn't cute. She had bad acne. Her face might have been cute if she had tried to make it cute, but when she shot her eyes at me in that WTW look, she was mad, and I guess if you never let anybody see your face, you would have no reason to try and make it attractive by using acne cream or lotion or makeup. She was just a warm body...a warm body who was annoyed with me. But it was a start. I would have put money on the fact that she hadn't looked at anyone else that day. So, that made me special. There were a couple of other times when I got her to look— not talk—but I was fighting a losing battle.

- - -

One day we finished football practice early because the

coaches had a meeting. I was parked around back by the practice field, and as I turned the corner to pass by the front of the school, I saw Danique sitting on the ground leaning up against the brick building like she was waiting for her ride. For some stupid reason, I did an illegal u-turn and drove into the lot and put the window down and asked if I could take her home. She didn't say anything, she just stood up, threw her bag on her shoulder, and walked over and got in on the passenger side. I was impressed! I hoped she realized that she was gonna have to talk to tell me how to get to her house, because I sure as heck didn't know where she lived! She told me the basics, "turn right; turn left," but she wasn't letting one extra word fall out of her mouth. I was just talking away, telling her about practice, how my day was, what I had for homework, that I was hungry, and it was a monologue.

We got to her house and it was pretty plain. It was small, brick, with a black front door, shrubs kind of grown up, grass kind of long, nothing really stood out. If it had been on a main road you could pass it every day and never look at it— kind of like Danique. Still not satisfied, I got out and took her bag off her lap and carried it up to the door with her. She took out her key and opened the front door. Just inside, with her head down, wearing a black hoodie over her head, she reached for her bag. I said, "Hey, I don't get invited in? I don't get a thank you! I don't even get a kiss good night?" We both stood there staring. I was staring at her and she was staring at…I don't know, my arm, or something. I couldn't tell 'cause her hair was over her eyes. It started to seem awkward, and I didn't know if somebody else was in the other room and was gonna come out popping caps, or if somebody was gonna pull in the yard and start something…so I just set her bag down. She mumbled, "thank you." Then I reached and hugged her. I meant for it to be quick, 'cause really I didn't know if I was about to get a beat down by the meanest dad in the world—the dad who forbade his daughter to look at a guy, a girl, a teacher, anything but her shoes. But the funniest thing happened...she embraced me back. She even laid her head on my chest a little. It was real sweet. It was like she hadn't been hugged in a while, or something. I rubbed her back a little and for the first time, *I* was a loss for words. Me! I was speechless! Finally, I said, "It's okay, Danique. I'm not gonna hurt you. You can trust me. I just wanna be your friend. You keeping everything bottled up inside, like nobody exists but you, that's not healthy. I bet you haven't said three words all day except to me. Am I right?"

She nodded her head.

"Well, that's not good. I know you got thoughts and feelings, and you need to talk to people. We don't bite. I don't anyway. You got a cell phone?"

She nodded, still looking down.

"What's your number? I'm gonna call you tonight."

She told me the number, and I immediately called her so she could save my number to her phone, too. I reached my arms out for another hug and she stepped closer to me and embraced me. I patted her back and told her I'd call her in a little while.

I got in the car and my mind was in WOW mode! I couldn't believe the progress I had made. I talked to a couple different girls as I drove home, nothing serious, just the usual. My mom called wanting me to stop and get some milk, and while I was in the grocery store I got a text...from Danique. Hey, thnx for bring me home. Nobody else here. Tryna find something to eat...Real thirsty. i got a lot of hw. Who do we play Friday? Are u gonna

37

score? Do lot ppl come to the games? I never been to 1. Do u like Littles? Looks funny to me...talks funny too. Sorry i don't look in ur eyes. Shy...scared. Stupid right? Thanks for everything...Hug 2. Needed that. C u tomor. I was like, DANG GIRL, don't you have a 120 character limit? Anyway, that was the start of it all. We talked that night, and the next day in class. I could see the shock on Mrs. Littles' face! And as it turned out, Danique wasn't short on words, she was just totally reserved. She talked to me and only me at school. If I didn't seek her out at lunch, she stood alone on the outside of the cafeteria and ate her lunch. She was strange. But she was also very sweet and funny. She was sarcastic, too. Her humor was very intellectual, not the norm. I had been scooting my stool over to lean against her arm, but once she and I started talking, I didn't do that anymore, and I think...she missed me, 'cause she started scooting over towards me!

Well, that got my masculine mind to thinking. Hmmm, she let me see her face, I wonder what else she might let me see. She liked my hug, so she likes my touch. And her face, the first time I saw it, it didn't do anything for me, but now, her eyes just lit up when she looked at me. It was as if she'd been looking *for* me. And she's not that bad looking, a seven, maybe. If she would dress herself up, pull her hair back, have some confidence, she might be an eight or nine! Some of my friends had seen me talking to her and they were confused about how I was able to get her to talk. Some of them tried to say bad things about her. They said she might have the cooties, or she might be the devil, but I chocked it up to fear of the unknown. If Danique was anything, she was unknown. When Danique and I embraced, it seemed like she wanted more from me, like she didn't want to let go...like she needed me. And I knew she did, she lived with her aunt. Her mom died last year and she had to move here with her aunt, and her aunt worked second shift, so she was always alone in the evenings, and she didn't have a driver's license. Our hugs had progressed to the point that we hugged several times a day. If I didn't take her home, I would stop by her house in the afternoon. Basically, she was my girlfriend.

- - -

Okay, so I was a virgin, and I was not proud of it. I had been lying about that for a while. My boys all thought I was the first to hit it—because that's what I told them. Then my stories got wilder and wilder to the point there was no way I could take it back. Lol. Well, it was my dream not to have to lie anymore. I wanted to tell the guys about one that was true. And I saw Danique as my chance.

I showered after practice and stopped by her house before I went home. When she opened the door, I walked in and just started kissing her…she was holding me tight. Her face was up to mine, and…our teeth kept clanking into each other's, and OMG! I was so ready for her! She had on a t-shirt and some shorts, not the usual, long-sleeved hoodie, like she wore at school. I pushed her hair back out of her face, and I told her I loved her. And that was probably true. I was becoming very protective of her, defending her when people said bad things about her and stuff. We were good friends. I had confided some things in her, and she had CERTAINLY confided in me. Her aunt had cooked, so she fixed me a plate and heated it up. I called my mom to tell her where I was. We ate and talked and watched TV for a little while. Sitting in the living room, I started feeling like I needed another kiss— or something, so I leaned towards her and she took my cue. We were kissing and I had pushed her down and was lying on top of her pressing her in to the sofa beneath us. She kept pushing my shoulders back and making sounds, but I wouldn't let up, I knew she was enjoying it. My whole body was ready—even my spirit was ready for what would come next. To make a good story respectable, we didn't do what I was hoping, but I did go home feeling real good.

Stopping by before I went home became a ritual over the next few weeks. My mom kept asking who I was visiting with and she wanted to meet the lucky girl, but I wasn't ready for that. She kept reminding me on sly that she wanted me to wait and have sex when I was married. I would always stop her in her tracks by asking a question that she didn't want to answer. She got embarrassed real easy.

I would stop by Danique's and eat and talk, and I would leave feeling good. Somehow, I guess I was greedy. I wanted to actually DO IT. We were exclusive. I knew I wasn't with anyone else, and I KNEW she wasn't with anyone else, so I didn't understand why she got shy on me when I mentioned taking things to the next logical step. It was like I was talking to the Danique I first met, the one with nothing to say, she wouldn't look me in the eye... After a few days it started to make me mad that she was acting like that. I hadn't done her wrong. I hadn't given her any reason not to trust me. So, why was she acting like this? I knew girls were supposed to play that quiet, shy role, but I couldn't understand why she was doing this to me? We were in love. Right?

One night, we started with our usual kissing...and I suddenly just stopped and asked her. "Can we please go all the way tonight?"

She started crying and said, "No."

I started rubbing her arm and I wiped her tears. "Why

not?" I begged.

She looked me right in the eyes with tears still streaming down her face. She was crying like she could hardly breathe, but she managed to say the following sentence that is not etched into my heart forever. She said, "I have HIV and I don't know how that will work."

Looking into her eyes, she became a monster. I mean, I even heard the roar of the monster! The room started spinning. I thought my life was coming to an end. I thought I was dying. I felt nauseous. I felt like I was shriveling up. My manhood began to ache like she had kicked me in the nuts! It was worse than any blue balls I had ever felt. I wanted to kill her. She let this thing go too far! Why didn't she tell me this a long time ago, like before she let me kiss her? God!

I stood up and she was crying out of control. She ran to the bathroom and slammed the door. I stood there with my whole life passing before my eyes. I've been kissing someone with HIV. OMG! How am I going to tell my mom this? I was enraged! I wanted to leave before she came out of the bathroom for fear I might beat her to death! I guess she heard the door open and she came running out to me and grabbed my arm. "Rob, don't be mad! I was going to tell you! I...I...I couldn't! I love you! And I know you love me, and...please don't be mad!"

I yanked my arm away from her, "Don't touch me ever again! If you gave me that stuff, you're going to hell!" I tried to walk away, but she grabbed onto me again, trying to pull me back into the house off the porch. I stopped and just stared up at the sky, wondering how long I had to live—how much longer I would be able to enjoy those beautiful stars in the sky. She said, "Rob, I was born with it. My mom had it when she got pregnant, but she didn't know she had it until I tested positive. Hers was too far along when she started treatment, and she died last year. I've been on treatment since I was born, and mine is very well controlled. My doctor says it's like I don't even have it! I am heathy! You don't have it, Rob. I promise you...you don't. I'm safe for kissing and stuff, but I wanted to tell you before we did anything else—especially without a condom. But, Rob, you can't just leave me. I don't have anyone but you. And you can't tell anyone. I just keep to myself because this isn't the kind of thing that helps a person make friends. Rob, I know you're mad, but I promise, you don't have it. Don't leave me like this, please! I love you."

I was still fuming mad, but through all of that, it was like...I felt sorry for her. I was still staring up at the sky, but I wasn't pulling away from her any longer. I didn't look at her but I reached for her and she stepped closer and embraced me around the waist. I laid my head on hers and rubbed her back. "I love you, Danique." She was crying and I felt like crying, but I was too mad. I was shocked, I was scared, I was confused, I was feeling every bad emotion there is...even grief. I just held her, and tried to comfort her, and calm myself down, 'cause whatever happened next we were in it together.

I cried in the car, OMG, I cried like I wasn't even myself. She sent me a text. I wanted to tell you, but i didn no how...i was scared u would leave me... hate me. I need u in my life. Ur fine. i know u r. I love u. I wouldn't do anything 2 hurt u ok. I no ur mad & u have a right to be, but plz don't be mad 4ever. U home yet?

I didn't know what to reply, but I knew she needed a reply, so I just said, almost home...good nite. I didn't sleep at all that night, and the next day I cut first block to go to the health department for an HIV test. They gave me this annoying questionnaire to fill out and they drew a whole testtube full of blood out of my arm. Usually when I get blood drawn, I can't look at it, but this time, I was staring at it hoping it looked normal...red...and nothing else...please nothing else!

They said it would be a week before they got my results. That was the LONGEST week of my life. She and I were still talking everyday and I was still visiting with her, but there was no kissing or anything else. It surprised me that even with this revelation, I didn't look at her any differently. She assured me that the virus was not affecting her health, it was just very difficult to tell people about it because they didn't understand. They jumped to conclusions and acted like they could get it from eye-contact. She told me about her last school and how the kids made her life hell because some of them knew her mother had HIV, so when she moved here, she decided to make herself invisible. She was my support for the week as I awaited my test results. On the following Thursday, she went with me to find out the verdict. When that lady said NEGATIVE, to say I was relieved would be an understatement. I was thanking Jesus and God and the Holy Ghost! I wrapped my arms tight around Danique and she hugged my waist tight. She and I are friends for LIFE! I still wish she had told me before we kissed or did anything else, but I do share in the blame for that, because I started it. I was being selfish. I was trying to lose my virginity, and I saw her as an opportunity. And now, as happy as I am to be negative, I am just as unhappy that she is positive. She's a good person, a good friend—now a friend of my friends, too, and she's my girl...my girlfriend...and I love her. I really do love her.

Think About It:

6-1 What emotions did you feel as you read this story?

6-2 Did you think Rob was to blame for his HIV scare? Why or why not?

6-3 Did you think Danique was to blame for Rob's HIV scare? Why or why not?

6-4 Did you see any of yourself in Rob?

6-5 Were Rob's motives in starting a friendship with Danique pure?

6-6 Can you determine a person's HIV status from just looking at them? What about other STDs?

6-7 Were you relieved when Rob was HIV-negative? How would you (and he) have felt if he had been HIV-positive? Was there a chance that he could have been HIV-positive? Danique assured him that she was safe...

6-8 In what ways did Rob exhibit responsibility or self-control?

6-9 For you, what was the take-home message from this story?

Quote by Charles Darwin from www.brainyquote.com accessed June 12, 2016

Sex lies at the root of life, and we can never learn to reverence life until we know how to understand sex.

Havelock Ellis

7 ~ Why Have Sex?

The answer to the title question is not as obvious as it may seem. Contrary to its most common use, which is pleasure, or secondary uses—to assert oneself as an adult, to achieve status among one's peers, to express the love felt in a romantic relationship—the purpose of sex or sexual intercourse, is to produce a baby. The purpose of sex is reproduction. Some animals, lower hierarchical animals, can reproduce sexually or asexually. Asexual reproduction is where a single parent produces a clone of itself by budding or regeneration. The problem with asexual reproduction is that the offspring carry the same genetic flaws that may lead to the death of the parent. Larger, more complex animals, mammals, reptiles, birds, and the like, only reproduce sexually. Sexual reproduction requires two parents whose genetic material combines to form the genetic makeup of their offspring. This genetic assortment is advantageous because potentially the offspring will be better suited to the environment, thus stronger and more survivable than its parents.

Sexual intercourse is the physical means of bringing

the male sex cell, sperm, into the female's birth canal (the vagina) near her reproductive cells, the eggs. The purpose of sexual intercourse is to unite the egg and sperm cell so that in 270 days (9 months), a new baby will be born, and the human race will continue. In other words, the purpose of sex is to create new life. Of course, every time two people have sex, it does not result in pregnancy, for a number of reasons, but the reason the male's anatomy fits into the female's anatomy is to bring sperm cells closer to egg cells, to increase the chances of reproduction. Testosterone causes the desire, then the pleasure factor keeps us coming back for more—pun not intended. ☺

The reproductive anatomy lends itself to reproductive success. The male's penis is shaped such that it fits into the vagina closer to the cervix (the opening to the uterus) where sperm can quickly reach the egg located inside the uterus. Sperm cells are the smallest cells in the human body, although their numbers are astronomical! Sperm cells have a tail, called a flagellum, that enables them to swim, but they need liquid through which to swim. Pre-ejaculatory fluid and vaginal fluids combine to give the sperm cells the perfect medium for swimming. The vaginal contractions, repeated tightening, and the male's pelvic thrusts work together to pull the sperm forcefully from the penis in through the cervix and closer to the egg. Both the penis and vaginal area are filled with nerve endings that make the act of sexual intercourse pleasurable—which entices us to do it frequently. The more often people have sex, the more likely they are to conceive a baby.

Even with the use of birth-control, the body can

achieve pregnancy. Any species that fails to reproduce will become extinct, so essentially there is a strong instinct or unconscious desire to procreate. Having a baby, producing new life, is not a task to take lightly. Babies grow into children, who grow into adolescents, who then become adults. Every person deserves to have two willful and deliberate parents working to ensure their safety, education, and spiritual growth. Babies should not be made haphazardly, pregnancy is not a spontaneous event! It is important to understand how the body works to achieve pregnancy, so that it can be prevented until the potential parents are ready. Although, at age thirteen, the body is ready to reproduce, sexual activity should be postponed until there is more mental and emotional maturity, financial readiness, and a willingness to nurture the next generation. In the face of peer pressure, testosterone, and one's own desires—self-control and good judgment must be the rule.

Think About It:

7-1 How would you have answered the question, *why have sex,* before reading this chapter?

7-2 After reading this chapter, what have you learned is the purpose of sex?

Quote by Havelock Ellis from www.brainyquote.com accessed on June 10, 2016

Courage is the most
important of all the virtues
because without courage, you
can't practice any other virtue
consistently.

Maya Angelou

8 ~ Party @ Lucky 8

I was sitting in US History class about to doze off 'cause Mr. Wilson was like the boringest teacher ever! He had the kind of voice that should be on a hypnosis recording. My notes were illegible, I was so sleepy from listening to him. My phone vibrated in my pocket and I jumped, mainly 'cause it scared me, but also I needed to press a key to stop it from making a sound so I wouldn't get it taken. When I had a minute I read the text.

Party @Lucky 8
on Cedar Ave Friday night.
$5. Food & Security.
FWD to 5 friends.

I rolled my eyes. I knew I wasn't going 'cause my mom wasn't about to let me go to any party at a hotel or any party that seemed like it was open to the public. I had two more years before I was a college student and I thought I could make my own decisions about what was safe, or better yet, what was *good* for me. But, my mom was a single parent to me and my sister, and it seemed like she tried to overdo it. It seemed like she was out to prove everybody wrong, that she could, against the odds, single-handedly keep us in order and out of trouble. She and my dad divorced when I was in fourth grade and it was hard on her at first, but she was determined to raise us without his input. When I was in middle school I gave her a little bit of trouble and he wanted me to come live with him. I kinda wanted to go live with him, too, but my mom was dead set against it. And now it seems like she's out to prove to him that she can get me out of high school and into college with no problems. But that means she's like super mean to me. Everything I ask her, she says no. Most of the time she doesn't even consider what I'm asking first, sometimes she won't even let me get the whole question out of my mouth and she's already telling me no. "What you need to do is get in there and get your homework done. You know you got football practice tomorrow and a game Friday night, I know you got some kinda test next week, now, don't be waiting 'til the last minute to start studying. Don't ask me about going anywhere!" That was her speech.

And another thing, I had been carrying my driver's permit in my wallet for six months beyond what was required. I could have tried for my license a LONG time ago, but she wouldn't let me. And I know why…'cause if I had my license I would be harder to keep up with, so that was her way of keeping me where she wanted me. She let me drive a lot and I was a good driver, but legally I couldn't drive by myself. Ugh!!!

Anyway, Friday night came around and we had a football game, we won, too! During the game my buddy Dwayne and I were talking about the party because he had got the text, too. I figured if I asked my mom if I could spend the night with him, his brother could drive us to the party. I texted my mom to ask her about spending the night and I told her I had a change of clothes with me already, she texted back. "I guess so. I gotta be at church at 9 to help get ready for carnival. What are u 2 planning"

I replied, "We r partners 4 project in sci...gotta work on it."

She replied, "On a Friday night?"

"Lol...yes mam."

"Okay...well, do u need any supplies? any $?"

I said, "He has supplies, but $ would be good so I can pay him back."

She texted, "Look 4 me after game."

I replied, "Thx!"

After the game, she was there and gave me two ten dollar bills out through the car window. She reminded me to mind my manners, not to be greedy, and to do my part on the project since we would be graded jointly. I nodded and said okay.

At Dwayne's house we showered and dressed to head out. We told his mom we were all three going to another guy, Nick's house for a little birthday party after the football game. That story was partly true...it was Nick's birthday and we were going to see him, but not at his house. He was coming to the Lucky 8 along with us.

When we arrived at the hotel, everything looked quiet and normal, but we could see there were more cars parked around towards the back than up near the lobby door. Around back there was a guy leaning against the brick wall with his legs crossed, texting on his phone. When he saw the car, he started signaling us to a park.

We got out straightening our clothes and checking each other out. I know I was nervous, but I tried not to show it. Nick walked in front of us, and I was third, right in front of Dwayne's brother Randy. The dude at the door shook hands with all of us and reminded us that it was $5 to come in. He let us in through a door that had a sign stuck to it that read *Door Locked at All Times Enter Through the Lobby*.

Just inside we were at the party room. They had rearranged everything and had somebody sitting at the door collecting the money. There were a lot of people packed in there and it was smoky. Some of the people were my age, but some were like 20 or so. There was music playing, but not too loud, I guess so the hotel staff wouldn't know there was a big party going on. There was a table with some doughnuts and a cooler with some sodas and beers in half-melted ice. Nick grabbed a beer and drank some of it, but not all. We were all kind of staying together, like we were scared or something. I wasn't scared, but I was nervous, being that I wasn't where I told my mom I would be, and the hotel didn't know this was going on. Basically, I knew if I got caught in there, my freedom as a sixteen year-old would never be the same. But, I didn't wanna seem uncomfortable, so I tried to relax, and break away from the guys I came with and either dance or find a girl to talk to. I grabbed a Cola, yeah Cola, not Coke out of the cooler and popped it open. That's when I realized, there were more party rooms adjoined to the one we originally entered.

I bumped Dwayne on the shoulder and we headed to the next room. There was a girl we knew from school, and we started talking to her, and from the way Dwayne started stepping over in front of me, I took that to mean he wanted me to take a hike, so I did.

I could hear that the next adjoined room was kinda happening from all the noise, so I made my way through the growing crowd over that way. That room was much darker, and the air was thick, it was sweaty, and it seemed like it was nothing but dudes in there. Most of them had a beer in their hand or they were smoking, and some had taken off their shirts, and had on undershirts and wife-beaters and they were laughing, and slugging each other around. The deep voices erupted in laughter and some of the guys kind of separated giving me a front row look at the main feature. A girl, maybe a woman, was on the bed wearing a thong and a bra and she was apparently taking requests, 'cause she had dollar bills hanging out of each of her two pieces of clothing. I stood there watching as they reached and grabbed her to turn her in their direction, to make them happy. I was conscious of the fact that I needed to keep my lips closed, 'cause I was shocked, but I didn't want to look like I was shocked. She was theirs for the taking. Some were paying some weren't, but she wasn't saying no to anyone.

I KNEW I didn't need to be there. I KNEW I should be moseying on along. I KNEW this was wrong. I KNEW I was expected not to just stand there, but to join in. My eyes, I'm sure, were as big as ping-pong balls both from adjusting to the darkness, and from what I was watching, but I didn't want to seem juvenile or embarrassed, although I was, so I decided to stay for a minute. I stayed for a few exchanges, then, after this one big dude was getting his congratulations and high-fives, I slipped out.

My heart was about to beat out of my chest. I found

Dwayne and Nick, and hit them on the shoulder as I walked by. Outside, in the cool air, I leaned against the car. I didn't care how long it took them to come out, I knew I wasn't going back in there. I stood there thinking about how my knowledge of sex had just changed. I knew about sex, but seeing it, and seeing that girl with all those dudes, was just…just not the way I pictured it to be. I knew that, to girls, sex was more special than it was to guys. I even knew some guys who had a bet going about who would lose their virginity first. I wasn't in the bet, but I could have lost my virginity a few minutes ago, but I didn't. I didn't want to. Part of me felt like I was crazy for passing up the opportunity, but then part or me was glad that I didn't. And another part of me felt really bad for that girl. I couldn't figure out why she would do that with all those eyes on her, for a few dollar bills? I thought she must not care anything about herself, and that thought made me sad. These testosterone-raging, high-fiving, sweaty, yelling dudes were taking full advantage of her. Standing there by the car, I realized that the guys in there had low self-respect, too. My mom talked about self-respect all the time and I thought I understood it, but it wasn't until that experience that I really understood it. I realized that my virginity was nothing to be ashamed of—that life would come in stages. "In due time," was something I had heard old folks say and that made sense now. I was sixteen with my whole life ahead of me to graduate, go to college, play football there and maybe play in the NFL! I still had a lot to learn but in the meantime, I had to stay healthy and not get any STDs or get anyone pregnant that would stop my progress.

Another thing I had heard, that now made sense, was about doing things, "in order." In order meant graduate high school, go to college, date, get engaged, get married, then have sex and have children. Out of order was what I just witnessed.

I was kind of in a hurry to lose my virginity, but that experience helped me to put that in perspective. I could, but it would be a big sacrifice and risk. By the time, Dwayne, Nick and Randy came out, it seemed like my decision not to have sex had made me a man.

Think About It:

8-1 How many lies did the narrator tell in order to arrive at the party?

8-2 Did you see any of yourself in the main character?

8-3 While following the crowd may be popular, is it always the best thing to do?

8-4 In what ways did the main character exhibit good judgment and self-control?

8-5 How did the narrators' final thoughts make you feel? Did you agree with any of his thoughts?

Your belief determines your action and your action determines your results. Make sure you can live with the results of your actions.

Carlos Wallace

9 ~ Child Support

Having a baby means bringing a new person into the world. That new person requires love, care, tenderness and nurturing in order to grow into a well-adjusted human being. Human babies are born helpless. The babies of horses walk a few minutes after they are born. Baby sea turtles hatch without any parents nearby. Their instinct is to head towards the sea, quickly before they are eaten by the predatory crab waiting nearby. About the only instinct human babies have is the instinct to suck. This is so that they can begin eating immediately, but someone who cares for them must be available to give them milk. Newborns cannot hold their own bottle. A newborn baby who feels cold, although lying next to his blanket, will not reach for it. A baby lying next to a tiger would not fear it, nor be able to get away from it. Human babies are absolutely helpless.

Whether maternal instincts do truly exist or not is up for debate, but females generally have some knowledge and expectation of the needs of a young child. Some fathers, on the other hand, do not. This lack of realization seems to be more common in fathers who did not intend to become fathers. Any man who is not ready to become a father, should not be sexually active. Too many fathers think they are fulfilling their responsibility of fatherhood by paying child support, but there are many things these men fail to realize. Babies don't spend money. Babies require things that must be purchased, but babies themselves, don't spend money. Children usually bear no financial knowledge until they reach ten or eleven years of age.

Newborns rely upon willing caregivers, usually their parents, to nurture them. Babies do not shop for their formula, clothes, change their own diapers, drive themselves to the doctor, make decisions about their education, sleeping habits, or room temperature. Their parents are supposed to do all of these things for them. Ask any parent about the first months of their child's life, and they will tell you that it was a struggle. Babies do not know night from day, they eat every two hours, they must be burped or they cry from gas accumulating in their tummy. And their diapers! Whew! At two in the morning! Child support payments do not cover these aspects of parenting.

Babies have physiological needs that are not always obvious, and babies can't talk to express these needs. It takes a mature, willing adult to recognize the needs of a baby. Parents who became parents unwillingly—like through birth control failure or unprotected sex, tend not be as willing. Unwilling parents tend to try to multi-task at inopportune times, which potentially dangers the life of their child.

Babies have psychological needs upon which their survival depends. As babies grow, they need to feel safe and secure. They need to feel consistency and constancy within the arms that cradle them. Babies, some say, have a sixth sense—the sense of security. When their parent or primary caregiver is unstable, insecure, or unwilling, they realize this and their development can be harmed. Babies are oblivious to child support.

Teens often lack the maturity to tend to a baby in a timely fashion, which can harm the baby's sense of security. When a baby is neglected, intentionally or unintentionally, his or her future psychological development can be greatly harmed. This damage cannot be repaired by a child support payment. The child may grow into an adult that requires years of professional counseling due to growing up feeling neglected.

Now, guys, be sure you understand the point of this chapter—the point is <u>not</u> that child support payments are unnecessary, but that <u>child support payments are not the end of your responsibility</u>. Support is an action word. It involves doing. Yes, child support payments are extremely helpful, and required by law. Child support payments, however, are not a good substitute for your presence as a father who loves and nurtures the development of his child. A man who is not ready to support his child by physically and emotionally being there for him should not have sex—children are frequently an unexpected result of sexual activity. Remember, the purpose of sex is to produce new life.

You likely know a father who is not regularly a part of his children's lives. There are many reasons why this may be the case, but by design, females cannot conceive a child alone. If females cannot make babies alone, it is probably not best for them to raise children alone. Fathers are important for helping children develop into mature, balanced individuals. "The presence of a father has a positive impact in many ways, as children with fathers have fewer behavioral problems, obtain better academic results, and are economically better off."[Why]

Because it is through sexual intercourse that humans reproduce, anytime people engage in sexual intercourse, it should be willful and responsible, and it should be with the knowledge that a baby could result. Again, testosterone may be a major driving force, but self-control and good judgment must take precedence over primal desires and instincts.

Think About It:

9-1 What was the author's purpose in this chapter?

9-2 Why isn't child support enough?

9-3 What is always the possible result of sexual activity?

Quote by Carlos Wallace from http://www.goodreads.com accessed June 10, 2016

Why Dads Matter. (n.d.). Retrieved December 29, 2011, from http://www.fathersforgood.org/ffg/en/fathers_essential/matter.html

Act as if what you do makes a difference. It does.

William James

10 ~ My Son

Donna wasn't my girlfriend, we just hooked up from time to time, usually at parties, or after a game or something. I mean, she was cool, I just wasn't trying to be tied down to anybody right then. She liked me and was all excited that I liked her, and she was telling people that we were more than we really were.

And now, my son, he's ten months old. He's like the most important person in my life. I might not become a successful person in the world, but I'm gonna make sure he has what he needs to be the best. I didn't know that fatherhood would make me mature like this all of a sudden, but when Devin spends the night with me and my mom and stepdad, I just hold him and kiss his little forehead. He's trying to walk a little bit, but it's going to be a while, I think. He was a little late at a few things—like he didn't start holding his head and neck until he was about 4 months old. Now, when I stand him up on my lap, he's still kind of weak around the knees, and his right foot turns outward. The doctor showed us some massages to do on him everyday that should help kind of mold his bones to a normal position and probably once he starts walking he'll need some physical therapy. He has Cerebral Palsy. I hate that for him, but he's a fighter. He's smart. I can see it in his eyes. The doctors don't know exactly what caused his condition, but…I think I know.

I heard the rumor before she told me, and that made me really mad. Somebody was like, "I hear you 'bout to be a baby-daddy." I was like *what the…?* And somebody else was like, "I hear you 'bout to have a birthday party…" I was confused, but then again, I was like I don't know what's going on, but she better step to me right! She can't be telling people anything without me knowing it. And I remember that whole week was bad, I had got put on probation at work for not cleaning the bathroom, but signing the log. I didn't apply to work at that Burger Kingdom to be cleaning the bathrooms. I was planning on fixing orders, and maybe cooking, but not cleaning bathrooms—especially not the men's room! So, I just went in there and flushed the toilets, 'cause that was all I could stomach. Then somebody complained and my manager went in there and my initials were on the log from like six minutes ago… And my car had been repossessed. I was already struggling to keep the insurance up, so everything was just going bad. Then this.

We were standing in the hall by the lockers on A-wing, I texted her to come to my locker after 4th block. When she came walking up I had just slammed my locker and she was standing there with this strange look on her face. I couldn't tell if she was scared, nervous, or what. I just asked her, what this rumor was I kept hearing, and she started crying and she said, "It wasn't supposed to become a rumor, I just told Anaya and it was supposed to be in confidence. But…yeah, I'm late…And I'm never late, so…that means you." I don't know what came over me, but I reached out and grabbed her around the neck and started choking her. Then I pushed her to the floor and she fell on her bookbag she had strapped onto her shoulders. I started walking away and she was crying and coughing and trying to yell at me. I didn't want to hear anything else she had to say. "She was like BJ! BJ! Is that how it's gonna be? Is that the kind of man you are?" It was all I could do to just keep walking and not go back and kick the hell out of her.

Well, I started shutting down. I didn't want to talk to anybody. My mom kept asking me what was going on...I didn't want to eat. I didn't want to find another job, although I knew I needed to be working overtime. I couldn't concentrate in my classes and people kept nudging me with their little comments and...I just had this rage building up in me. And nothing could stop it. This was not supposed to happen. She and I weren't talking all that much anymore, but when we did, ugh, I hated her! I hated the sound of her voice, the look in her eyes, and most of all, that big belly she was getting. She didn't look pregnant from the back, but from the front, it looked like she had eaten a Thanksgiving turkey whole! I had some doubts that the baby was mine, but I had been there, so she was probably right.

One day we were at school and she was telling me something about...I don't even know, she was just annoying me like crazy, and this uncontrollable rage started coming over me, like I could hardly breathe. We were walking down the steps and nobody else was in the stairwell, and she was about two steps down in front of me and I reached out and pushed her down the last three or four steps. With that bookbag on her back, and that big stomach, she lost her balance and went flying down the steps and she hit her head on the wall. She was down there in this weird position crying and holding her stomach. I just walked away.

If I regret anything I ever did in my life it was that I did those things to Donna while she was pregnant—or that I *ever* did that to her. And those were just some examples, there was more. I was more than a dead-beat-dad, I was a freaked-out-father-to-be. And now my son has to live in the shadow of my wrongs. I hate to admit it, and it's not an excuse, but of the few memories I have of my parents together, it was my dad hurting my mom. He went to jail for a while. He's out now, but he doesn't come around. I don't want to be like him. I want to be the opposite. I know what I missed out on without a father and I can't do that to Devin. I should have talked to somebody about my feelings instead of letting it boil over when she started talking to me, trying to get me to own up to our future together. Devin looks just like me when I was a baby. The first time I looked at him all of the hardness in my heart just melted. My mom has some of my baby pictures in the living room and…there's no need for a DNA test, he is my son. I love him. I love Donna, too. We're not together, but she gave me the best thing that ever happened to me and I owe her big props for that, and for being a survivor to everything I did to her.

Think About It:

10-1 When you think of child support, what comes to mind?

10-2 What form of child support is the narrator giving to his son?

10-3 For you, what was the take-home message of this story?

**Our main reproductive
organ is our brain.**

Molly Kelly

11 ~ Wired

Somewhere in your life, you have probably heard the expression men are from Mars and women are from Venus. [Men] Or as a child you heard the nursery rhyme that indicated boys were made of snakes and snails and puppy dog tails, while little girls were made of sugar and spice and everything nice. It is true that males and females are different, but we are not from different planets, nor is one all good and the other all bad.

Men and women are made to complement each other. This means that the weaknesses of one must be abundant in the other, so that the partnership will work. It is estimated that the male brain is 11-12% larger than the female brain, but there is no evidence to support the fact that males are smarter than females.[Are Male] The larger brain, scientists believe, is a result of the fact that males have greater muscle mass, thus more neurons in the brain to control the additional muscles.

The brain is made of two hemispheres or sides, connected by the corpus callosum which is a band of nerves that help the two hemispheres to communicate. Females tend to have a larger corpus callosum.[Are There] The left hemisphere of the brain tends to function in analytical and logical thought processes such as speaking, calculating and reasoning, while the right hemisphere tends to function in intuition and dreams. It is the right brain that is responsible for body language, relationships, and creativity.[Are Male] Males tend to use more of their left-brain, while females, with their larger corpus callosum, have a greater ability to transfer information between hemispheres, thus accessing more brain capability at once. As you can see, males and females are wired differently.

Harvard professor, Edward O. Wilson, considered to be the father of sociobiology (a field that attempts to study the biological basis for psychological and sociological differences between males and females) made the following comparison, "Human females tend to be higher than males in empathy, verbal skills, social skills and security-seeking, among other things, while men tend to be higher in independence, dominance, spatial and mathematical skills, rank-related aggression, and other characteristics."[Are There]

Females tend to be empathetic and security-seeking, while males tend to be independent, dominant, and more aggressive. Females, traditionally known as the weaker sex, are then vulnerable to exploit by their male counterparts. Think about how that could happen. Ponder if you have ever taken advantage of the kindness of a female. Think about your sister, your female cousins, your mother—how would you feel if they were being exploited by a man? Remember that all of the girls you come in contact with are someone's sister, cousin, etc.

"**Hey, you can't do this to me! You already got me started, you can't stop like this! Have you ever heard of blue balls? You're gonna have me scarred for life! If I don't keep going, from this point, my whole groin will turn blue and you know that what means, no circulation, and I might have heart attack and die! And it will be your fault! Do you want that on your conscience?**" Blue balls carry absolutely no long term effects—no permanent discoloration due to lack of blood supply, no risk for heart attack, no death! Blue balls are a slang term for a condition characterized by vasocongestion in the genital area. When a man is aroused, the arteries in the genitals dilate to bring more blood to the testicles and the penis—at the same time the veins, which carry deoxygenated blood back to the heart—tighten to maintain the erection and level of arousal. If the arousal is followed by ejaculation, the reversal of blood flow proceeds without pain. If there is no ejaculation, it takes a few minutes for the arteries and veins to reverse the flow of blood, which is painful, but temporary. [Health] Unfortunately, it is common for young men to blame their female counterpart for the pain they are experiencing in attempt to make her give-in to sexual intercourse. Again, that female is someone's sister, cousin, etc. If she has already told you that she is not interested in sexual intercourse at that time, then it's wrong to blame her for your erection or your blue-balls.

"**Well, if you don't wanna go all the way, you could just...do it with your mouth. That way it won't be...real sex, and I won't die of blue balls.**" Have the two of you each discussed your definition of sex? People define sex in different ways, but for the purpose of this book let's define it as giving or receiving of ANY pleasurable feelings through physical contact with the genitals. Oral sex fits the definition—and so does the anal alternative. STDs can be transmitted through both oral and anal sex. Both alternatives, like "real sex" require a great deal of commitment and trust from both partners. If she is not in total agreement with the act, she can be left with feelings of guilt, shame, and resentment towards you, her male counterpart. Guilt because she compromised her true intentions; shame because she's embarrassed and she may resent you because you asked her to do it—and you claimed that you loved her. True love does not make uncomfortable requests. All forms of sex should be reserved for marriage.

"Why? Because I love you! And you say you love me? Sex is the next natural thing for us, unless you don't really love me. If you love me you'll prove it." Why should she have to prove her love for you by compromising her body? In what ways have you proven your love for her? Have you asked her father if he would be willing to allow you to marry his daughter? Have you asked her to marry you? Have you bought her a $5000 ring, and a $250,000 house to live in after you are married? Have you been absolutely honest with her? Do you put her needs before your own? If you are putting pressure on her to have sex with you, taking advantage of her desire to be loved and adored, in exchange for the safety and security she thinks you will provide, that's not love. Girls have nothing to prove to you.

There exists a double-standard in what males and females are taught about sex. Girls are taught resistance and guys are taught moderation. Virginity tends to be more precious to females than it is to males. Guys desire to lose their virginity, if not by prom night, then *on* prom night. Women, in some societies of the world, take drastic steps to give the appearance of virginity on their wedding night.

You have already read about some differences in the male and female brain; additionally it is believed that there are subconscious drives that make females more satisfied with a single partner for life, and males more prone to multiple partners. As explained earlier, there are billions of sperm cells in a single ejaculate—all competing for the chance to share DNA with an egg cell. The vast majority of sperm cells never fertilize an egg. But men produce sperm cells 24-hours a day. By mating with multiple females, it increases the chance that one of his sperm cells will fertilize an egg and carry on his genetic line. Females, on the other hand, tend to value monogamy (a single sexual partner) as they scrutinize potential males in search of the best genes from a dependable partner who will remain in her life to protect her and her offspring.[Moalem]

Having an awareness of some of the differences in how the brain of the opposite sex is structured, and how that structure influences thinking and reasoning should help you develop more meaningful relationships in the future. Sex can be any form of genital pleasure, and the desire to give or receive that pleasure should be mutual. Sex is a commitment in and of itself. The purpose of sexual intercourse is to produce offspring, so making the decision to have sex, is also the acceptance of potential parental responsibilities, if pregnancy results. Sex involves sharing body fluids which may contain viruses or bacteria with potential lifelong effects.

While testosterone may be the driving force towards sexuality, it must be checked with good judgment and self-control. Your good judgment should be aided by the knowledge gained in this book—the ability to see a situation for what it really is and what it could become.

Good judgment, means that you act within the acceptance of the consequences, and you don't take unnecessary risks. Casual sex always carries risks. Self-control is the test of good judgment. The benefits and risks have been weighed, but that pleasure factor—it is hard to ignore! Those blue balls...that stigma of still being a virgin after prom night...then there's the possibility of pregnancy, a STD, emotional pain, possible humiliation. Is it worth it?

Abstinence carries no risks. Sexually Transmitted Diseases are transmitted through sexual contact, not through abstinence. Babies are conceived through sexual intercourse, but not through abstinence. No female has <u>ever</u> harbored resentment for the guy who did not pressure her into sexual activity, but found just her company satisfying and rewarding. It is true that males and females are different. We are supposed to be different, but in complementary ways. Waiting to enter a sexual relationship—which requires good judgment and self-control, is one of the best ways to ensure that your relationships are healthy.

Think About It:

11-1 How do differences in the male and female brain make males and females function differently in relationships?

11-2 You've learned that the things you say to a girl can be very influential, is it fair to use her sympathetic and caring mind against her?

11-3 How is the decision to have sex a commitment?

Quote by Molly Kelly from www.azquotes.com accessed June 2, 2016

Men Are from Mars, Women Are from Venus Quotes by John Gray. (n.d.). Retrieved December 26, 2011, from https://www.goodreads.com/work/quotes/55001-men-are-from-mars-women-are-from-venus

Are Male and Female Brains Different? (n.d.). Retrieved November 26, 2010, from http://www.webmd.com/brain/features/how-male-female-brains-differ#2

Are There Differences between the Brains of Males and Females? (n.d.). Retrieved November 26, 2010, from http://www.cerebromente.org.br/n11/mente/eisntein/cerebro-homens.html

Health. (2005). Blue Balls. Retrieved November 26, 2010, from http://health.howstuffworks.com/sexual-health/male-reproductive-system/blue-balls-dictionary.htm

Moalem, S. (2009).How sex works: why we look, smell, taste, feel, and act the way we do. New York, NY: Harper.

A widespread taste for pornography means that nature is alerting us to some threat of extinction.

J. G. Ballard

12 ~ Por•nog•ra•phy

It used to be that men would secretly buy "men's magazines" to flip through during times when they were bored or lonely, but times have changed. Internet porn is a multi-billion dollar industry. Currently, at least 12% of Internet websites are pornographic.[The Stats] What is pornography? Pornography includes pictures, movies, or writing that show or describe sexual behavior for the purpose of exciting people sexually. [How]

Sometimes young men (and women) think of pornography as a good alternative to physical sex. They think it's a good alternative because it does not carry the risk of pregnancy or STDs, but it should not be considered harmless. In a previous chapter you read about how the human body needs to reproduce in order to avoid extinction. The genital area has thousands of nerve endings that make sex pleasurable. We like things that are pleasurable. We repeatedly do things that are pleasurable. Online pornography makes this pleasure easily accessible. Too easily accessible. While pornography may carry no risk of STDs or pregnancy, it does have its risks.

In an article titled, *Watching Pornography Damages Men's Brains*, author Sarah Knapton, explains that in men who report watching pornography, a part of the brain, the striatum, "which activates when people feel motivated or rewarded, shrinks and works less efficiently. So people who watch a lot of porn are likely to need increasingly graphic material to achieve the same sexual stimulation." [Knapton] Sixty-four men participated in this study. Think about it, watching porn causes a person to need more and more pornographic material in order to feel the same pleasure they felt the first few times they viewed it. It is also very unlikely that any true sexual encounter will measure up to what they have seen online. In other words, watching pornography can decrease the normally-amazing pleasure of actual sexual intercourse. Of the men who reported watching the most porn, when connected to a device to measure brain activity, they were not aroused by pictures of naked women. Have you ever heard of building up a tolerance for alcohol? Over time, it takes more alcohol to make a regular drinker reach the point of intoxication. It's the same idea with pornography. Just as alcohol is addicting, so is pornography.

Psychologists are reporting that the need for counselling due to pornography addiction is on the rise. In fact, they have identified two different forms of pornography addiction—Classic and Contemporary. Classic porn addicts who seek counselling are around age 28, and look at porn for 10 to 30 hours per week. (Think about that. A full-time job is usually 40 hours per week.) They seek counselling when they realize their life is in trouble—they can't keep a girlfriend (girls DO NOT like for their boyfriends to look at pornography), or they lose their job because they got caught looking at porn at work.

The other form of pornography addiction is called Contemporary. A Contemporary porn addict who seeks counselling is generally a "20-year-old male who started looking at porn when he was 12, just as puberty was kicking in. By age 14 he is using porn nightly. By age 15 he's quit sports and clubs, preferring to spend his time alone, looking at and masturbating to pornography. His once-good grades are terrible, he's lost contact with his friends, and he's never dated. Now, at 20, he's depressed, anxious, and ashamed about his life. He wants to do better in school and he wants to have friends and a normal romantic relationship, but he doesn't know how to make any of that happen. So he sticks with what he knows: the endless intensity of online pornography." [Weiss]

True, pornography does not carry the risks of pregnancy or STDs, but it can steal the pleasure out of the very thing you desire. Pornography is addictive. Pornography can ruin your life, and in the future it can ruin a marriage. Unfortunately, it is free and widely available. The only thing to prevent the damage is for you not to click on it. The way to stop yourself from clicking on it is to develop self-control. This chapter was included to give you important information to help you make better decisions. What constructive habits do you have? Do you draw? Do you write? Do you like to play basketball? Do those things and stay off the porn websites. You are the only person who can protect your future from the damage that viewing pornography can cause. Now that you have been informed, it is up to you to make decisions that will lead to happy and healthy relationships.

Think About It:

12-1 Does watching pornography carry any risks? Explain.

12-2 How does watching a little porn become a porn addiction?

12-3 What differences and similarities did you notice about the two categories of porn addicts?

12-4 List 4 reasons why a girlfriend (or wife) would be upset if she knew her boyfriend (or husband) were viewing pornography.

12-5 The author asks what constructive habits you have. List 5 constructive things you enjoy.

12-6 What does the quote at the start of this chapter mean? How is it true? "A widespread taste for pornography means that nature is alerting us to some threat of extinction." *J. G. Ballard*

Quote by J.G. Ballard from www.quoteland.com accessed January 4, 2017

The Stats on Internet Pornography [Infographic] | Daily Infographic. (2013, January 04). Retrieved January 05, 2017, from http://www.dailyinfographic.com/the-stats-on-internet-pornography-infographic

Knapton, S. (2014, May 24). Watching pornography damages men's brains. Retrieved January 05, 2017, from http://www.telegraph.co.uk/science/2016/03/14/watching-pornography-damages-mens-brains/

Weiss, R. (2016, September 29). Pornography: How Much Is Too Much? Retrieved January 05, 2017, from http://www.collective-evolution.com/2016/09/29/pornography-how-much-is-too-much/

The real man smiles in trouble,
gathers strength from distress, and
grows brave by reflection.

Thomas Paine

13 ~ Abuse

Victim #1

Now 22 years old, Aaron Fisher can more openly tell the story of his summer camp experiences through the Second Mile nonprofit organization. It was there that he met Pennsylvania State University's former Assistant Football Coach, Gerald "Jerry" Sandusky. He spend many nights in the older man's basement were pats on the thigh and kisses on the forehead became unmentionable sexual encounters.

"I didn't have any say in what I went through, but I did have the decision of what to do after," Aaron says. A total of eight victims testified at Sandusky's trial in 2012. While the others remained nameless, everyone knew the full identity of Victim #1. This forced him to endure gossip and ridicule in his small home town of Lock Haven, PA. He says he was plagued with thoughts of suicide and even attempted suicide, but thankfully was unsuccessful.

He has now coauthored a book, titled *Silent No More* to tell his story in his own words. He also speaks to groups, to "open the world's eyes to the epidemic of sexual abuse. [Durkel]

85

Juveniles Sexually Abused in Custody

His mother didn't say she was glad her son was sentenced to prison, but she admits that on his first night away, she "could sleep because he was safe." What she did not know was that shortly after he began his sentence, her 15 year-old son would become involved in a sexual relationship with the director of security at the state juvenile corrections center in Nampa, Idaho.

Later, the director of security, a 29 year-old woman, admitted to falling in love with the boy. She pleaded guilty to the charges of lewd acts with a minor and was sentenced to five to twenty years in prison.

A February 2016 article reports that as many as ten percent of children in detention are sexually abused. The abuse is often repeated by either female guards or other juvenile detainees. [Joaquin]

Sexual abuse happens. It happens to both males and females. It doesn't always make the news. The perpetrator is not always caught. The victim does not always report the abuse. An abuser does not always abuse multiple victims. Sexual abuse is real and it has long-lasting effects. Unfortunately, it happens every day.

Statistics indicate that 1 in 6 men have experienced some form of unwanted sexual contact at some point in their lives before the age of 18. Due to such high statistics, this chapter has been included in case you, or someone you know, has experienced abuse.

If you have experienced abuse, you must seek help. Tell someone you know and trust, or contact your local law enforcement. As you seek help, you must understand that your body can become sexually aroused even if your brain does not want it to react. Your body can have an involuntary response to certain types of contact. Your body's response does not mean that you liked the attention or wanted the attention. Your body's response does not mean that what happened was your fault. Sexual abuse is the fault of the abuser who seeks to take advantage of, manipulate, or misuse the relationship between himself or herself and the victim.

If you have been abused, you must realize that past abuse has nothing to do with how masculine you are. Many men who have been sexually abused report feelings of shame or guilt, and have symptoms of post-traumatic stress disorder. They feel shame because they believe they allowed themselves to be dominated, which is not something they believe "real men" should do. Men who have been sexually abused may feel more vulnerable than they believe a "real man" should feel. Understand that "real men," come in all different shapes, sizes, and all real men experience different thoughts, feelings, and emotions. Having experienced abuse, does not make or break one's masculinity.

Another common question that plagues the minds of men who have been sexually abused is the question of their own sexual identity. Having been sexually abused by a man does not automatically make a young man gay. Remember, the body can become sexually aroused even when the mind detests the act.

The point of this book is to empower young men with the self-control to postpone sexual relationships until marriage. Having been sexually abused can cause a young man to think he needs to prove his masculinity through a sexual relationship with a female, even if he is not married. The emotional pain sexual abuse is usually not healed by additional sexual partners. The pain of sexual abuse is aided by seeing the abuser brought to justice, by counselling, and through healthy, loving relationships. Everything in this book applies to both young men who have been abused and those who have not been abused. Healthy sexual relationships should take place within the bounds of marriage.

If you would like more information, go to <u>https://1in6.org.</u>

<u>Think About It:</u>

13-1 What thoughts did you have as you read the two opening articles?

13-2 In your opinion, what makes a man a *real man*?

13-3 Can you understand why having been abused might cause a young man to doubt his masculinity? Explain.

Quote by Thomas Paine from www.brainyquote.com accessed January 4, 2017

Facts & Myths. (n.d.). Retrieved December 27, 2016, from https://1in6.org/men/myths/

Dunkel, E. (2015). Victim 1 finds his voice. Retrieved August 24, 2016, from http://www.philly.com/philly/news/Victim_1_finds_his_voice.html

Joaquin Sapien / ProPublica. (n.d.). Why Are Rates of Sexual Abuse in Juvenile Detention Facilities on the Rise? Retrieved August 24, 2016, from http://www.alternet.org/education/why-are-rates-sexual-abuse-juvenile-detention-facilities-rise

Elinson, Z. (2015). Juveniles Sexually Abused by Staffers at Corrections Facilities. Retrieved August 29, 2016, from http://www.wsj.com/articles/juveniles-sexually-abused-by-staffers-at-corrections-facilities-1420160340

Knowing when to walk away is
wisdom.
Being able is courage.
Walking away, with your head held
high is dignity.

Unknown

14 ~ Walk Away

We moved two weeks before the start of school, so I was about to be the "new guy" at Fairview High. My dad took me to register for school, but I still didn't know anyone. Even in my neighborhood, I didn't see anyone my age.

For the first day of school, I didn't want to wear my new school clothes—too starched. I wanted to be chill and just try to fit in. As long as I had my Chapstick, I would be alright. There were two dudes at the bus stop, both of them were into their phones. Nobody even spoke. For two weeks I had been thinking about what school would be like. Now I was thinking about when I would get my driver's license. This was really awkward.

Finally the bus pulled up and we climbed on board. I found a seat about midway to sit by myself. At the next stop these girls got on the bus. One of them sat with me. She sat there like it was her assigned seat. The other two sat across the aisle. Now for some conversation! They wanted to know my name, where I was from…. They kept giving each other "the eye." Their eyes were getting really big and they were all smiling. I wasn't used to having this effect on so many girls at one time. As the bus turned into the school parking lot, we compared schedules. All of us were in 10th grade, but Leah would be moving up to 11th grade in January. I had Geometry with Leah, Art with Kayla, and PE with Mya 4th block. So far, so good.

The rest of my first day was pretty uneventful—four classes and lunch. It surprised me that we took yearbook pictures on the first day. That was new. It also surprised me that I had homework—in 3 classes! And we were expected to dress out in PE tomorrow or our grade would drop by a letter.

After school on the bus, it was me, Mya, Leah, and Kayla once again. This time, though, when Leah noticed Mya sitting next to me, she gave her a serious evil-eye. Instead of sitting across the aisle from us, like she did this morning, she came to our seat and sat on my lap and put her feet on Mya. She wrapped my arms around her and held them there while the rest of the kids got on the bus. I knew the bus driver was gonna say something, it was just a matter of time. She was holding tight to my hands to make sure her friends saw that we were "together." Then, I knew it… the driver looked up in that big rearview mirror and saw her sitting up high. She stood up and yelled, "Get off him! We ain't having no hanky-panky on this here bus!" Talk about embarrassing.

Leah got up and sat between me and Mya. A few minutes later she realized she was missing an earring. She started looking everywhere! She stood up, was feeling her pockets, wanted us to stand up and she patted us down. She felt my legs, my crotch, my stomach, my chest. Did I say my crotch? I laughed and tried to play it off, but…my manhood got the wrong message. I got one. I had to put my bookbag on my lap for the rest of the ride. I didn't realize we were almost at my stop. I had to stand up. Dang!

Then that night they started texting me, and yes, I was

texting them, too. I even got pictures of all of them. I'm not gonna say I didn't like the attention, because I did. It was new for me, but I liked it. My mom always said, anything too good to be true, probably is. I was a bit leery of where this was going, but I was willing to play along.

The second day of school was pretty good. I was pleasantly surprised at how much of the review in Geometry I remembered from Algebra. Geometry seemed like it would be pretty easy. It was PE, yeah PE, where I wasn't so sure. Don't get me wrong, I was athletic! I could bench 180 and my 40-yard time was under 6-seconds. I was pleasantly surprised to find that at Fairview High, males and females took PE together. This was new. At my old school, girls didn't take PE with the guys, I guess that's because health-ed, or really it's sex-ed, was a part of PE.

So, we all had to dress out. Most of the girls, except the thicker ones, had their shorts rolled up and they had tied or either cut their t-shirts to show their waistline and belly-button.

After jumping-jacks and up-downs, Coach Rogers told us to find a partner. Mya ran over and grabbed my arm. As Coach Rogers explained what was to come, she was hugging my arm to her chest and against her stomach. I tried to focus on Coach Rogers, but she wasn't making it easy for me. One thing I heard him say was that whoever we chose as a partner today would be our partner for the semester. Partners would help each other with stretches and would hold each other's feet for sit-ups. Okay.

So, I sat on the gym floor to start my stretches and Mya stood behind me. She was supposed to be pushing me forward, but she was massaging my shoulders. And then... we switched places for sit-ups, and I found out one more rule Fairview High didn't have for girls in PE. Underwear! I tried not to get caught looking. I think I made it through like 3 sit-ups. I couldn't stay in the gym. This was a bit much. I let go of her feet and went to the locker room. I just sat on the bench. Don't get me wrong, I liked what I saw, but not in PE! Not in class! Not like that! And she was gonna be my partner the whole semester!

It was only a few minutes before I heard the piercing sound of a whistle. "What are you doing in here?" It was Coach Rogers.

"I'm sorry, Coach. I need a new partner. That girl...that girl...I can't hold her legs like that everyday, that's all I'm gonna say."

"What? What's your name?"

"Darren Shore."

"You're new here, right?"

"Yes sir."

"I've told the administration we need to stop putting girls and boys together for PE, but they don't hear me. Don't worry about it, I'll get you a new partner. Do you want a male or a female?"

"I mean...a female, sir, but..."

"Look Darren, you've gotta understand that you are the new guy here. You've got the girls' hormones in a frenzy. They're all competing to be your girlfriend. I suspect your partner did something that got you worked up. Don't worry about it. That's not your fault. You did the right thing. Walk away. As you keep on living, you'll find that walking away is sometimes the best thing you can do!"

He continued, "These girls don't know what they're doing. The attention they get, is gonna be the wrong attention. Then they'll want to blame the guy. I've been teaching PE for 19 years and I've seen this trend with these aggressive girls. It really bothers me, too. When I was your age, we guys had to get up the nerve to make the first move, or ask the question to get the conversation started. And really, that's what made us men. We put our neck on the chopping block and sometimes it got cut off. But sometimes, things worked out. We took the chance on a girl. These girls, they come on strong. They take flirting to a whole new level. They lack self-control."

"Darren, you seem like a good kid. Don't let these girls make you lose your morals. I promise you, they'll try. You've gotta make your own mind up, and you've gotta set your own boundaries, and you've gotta be able to walk away—just like you did today! Keep thinking about your future. Walk away, man, I ain't mad at you. You did what you had to do. I'm proud of you. Let me know who you want your new partner to be. I'll make it happen."

Coach Rogers became my favorite teacher.

Think About It:

According to a study published in 2014, 43% of high school boys and young college men report having an unwanted sexual experience. Of those, 95% said a female acquaintance was the aggressor. [Fink]

14-1 Is pressure from a girl an appropriate reason to have sex?

14-2 Have you ever been the subject of unwanted attention from girls? How did you respond?

14-3 How did Darren demonstrate the use of self-control? Good judgement? Morality?

14-4 Coach Rogers said Darren did the right thing by walking away? In what other ways could he have responded?

14-5 The previous chapter discussed abuse. How is dealing with a sexually aggressive girl similar to abuse?

Quote by Unknown from www.lifehack.org accessed on January 13, 2017

Fink, J. L. (2016, May 09). Talking to Boys about Sexually Aggressive Girls. Retrieved January 14, 2017, from https://buildingboys.net/talking-boys-sexually-aggressive-girls/

Sexual intercourse is a gift
that says,
"Do not open until marriage."
If you've already unwrapped it,
wrap it up again!

Molly Kelly

15 ~ Secondary Virginity

"Um...I know it's absurd, but...what if I'm reading this book and beginning to regret losing my virginity? Too late, right?" Absolutely not! You can always stop doing something you later realize is not good for you. They say bad habits are *hard* to break, not *impossible* to break. Like making the decision to stop mouthing off to your mom, or to stop biting your fingernails, or to stop using profanity, you have to make a firm decision and get to work on making the change. If you have a girlfriend, with whom you are sexually active, you must explain to her that abstinence is important to you. Then you must stop allowing yourself to be in situations where sex is convenient or imminent. Mostly likely, she will understand your decision and honor you for sticking to it.

As with most big changes we attempt to make in our lives, it is more easily done with the support of people who care. If you are seeking secondary virginity, surround yourself with friends who are virgins—not virgins-in-waiting, but friends who are committed to abstinence. Their support will give you the strength you need to withstand the seemingly overwhelming pressures to be sexually active. If you cannot find friends that fit the aforementioned description, talk with an adult—your parents, your youth minister—they will understand and they will help you to be accountable.

It is never too late to make a decision for good. Whether you have had one sexual partner, or seven, if you decide that enough is enough, then it is up to you stand firm in your decision. Do not be fooled in thinking that just because you make the decision, that all of your sexual desires will just go away—they will not. As long as you are healthy and normal, those feelings will remain. You have to be stronger than your testosterone. You must think in terms of pros and cons, risks and benefits, and make decisions that are beneficial and healthy into the future.

Think About It:

15-1 Think of a bad habit you have broken. How did you do it? Why did you make the decision to do it?

15-2 Think of someone who has quit smoking. Do you think they will ever be tempted by cigarettes again? How should they deal with the temptation?

15-3 If you are seeking secondary virginity, how will you handle sexual temptation in the future?

Quote by Molly Kelly from www.azquotes.com accessed on June 10, 2016

Integrity is choosing your thoughts and actions based on values rather than on personal gain.

Chris Karcher

16 ~ True Story

Many, many years ago there lived a king named David. His soldiers were at battle, and he was supposed to be at battle, as well. Instead, he sent his assistant, Joab, out with the army. One evening while David was out on the roof of his palace, his attention was struck by a beautiful woman who was bathing down below. David could take neither his eyes nor his mind off of her. He sent one of his servants to find out who she was. His servant reported back that her name was Bathsheba, the daughter of Eliam, and the wife of Uriah. David, being the king, knew that Uriah was away at battle, so he had plenty of time to spend with Bathsheba while her husband was away. He sent for her and slept with her.

Soon Bathsheba realized that she was pregnant. David didn't know what to do and was afraid of her husband's reaction. He decided that he would call Uriah home from battle for some bogus reason. He figured while he was at home he could sleep with his wife and would think that the baby was his.

David sent word to Joab advising that Uriah should report to him immediately. When Uriah arrived, David asked him questions about how the war was progressing. Uriah responded, then David sent him to his house to get washed up. Hoping to make the time with his wife more special, King David sent him a gift. To his dismay, his servant reported that Uriah did not go to his house. He, instead, slept among the servants. On the following day, David wasted more of Uriah's time with questions about the war then sent him home. Again, Uriah did not go to his house, he slept among the servants. On the third day, David asked him why he had not gone to his house. Uriah explained that to go home and be with his wife would not be fair to his military comrades who were still away at battle. Instead of going home to his wife he decided to suffer without her as his comrades were suffering without their wives. Uriah returned to battle.

King David felt that he was running out of options, so he sent word to Joab to relocate Uriah to the front-line of battle so that he would surely be killed. Several days later, Joab sent word to David telling him that Uriah was dead. David told Bathsheba the news of her husband's death and she mourned for him.

Soon Bathsheba married David and gave birth to a son. Shortly after his birth, the child was struck with an illness. David pleaded with God to save his child as he fasted and prayed. After seven days, the child died.

Think About It:

16-1 What examples of self-control did you find in the story?

16-2   To lack self-control is to be undisciplined, mischievous, or defiant. What examples of the lack of self-control were in the story?

16-3   Which character, David or Uriah, are you most like? Explain.

16-4   In what way(s) can the lack of self-control lead to a person's demise?

16-5   Which character exhibited integrity? In what ways?

We must allow the Word of God to confront us, to disturb our security, to undermine our complacency and to overthrow our patterns of thought and behavior.

John R. W. Scott

17 ~ God's Word

Can you guess where the story of David and Bathsheba came from—Greek folklore, Aesop's Fables, a talkshow—No! That story is found in the eleventh and twelfth chapters of 2 Samuel. That story is in the Bible and it is true. The story contains a contrast of two men. One who makes poor decisions, uses bad judgment and has no self-control. The other man uses good judgment and demonstrates self-control. King David was not a wicked man with no morals, he knew he had made a mistake and didn't want to cause further hurt, so he sent for Uriah to come home and be with his wife. When that didn't work he had him killed. His widow mourned and I'm sure he mourned with her, as he was under a great deal of stress. He later married her. There is no passage about any love he felt for her or commitment to her, so it is possible that their marriage was like more of an appeasement. It does seem that David loved his child. Later their child developed an illness, David pleaded with God, but the child still died. David wasn't an immoral person, he did immoral things—like many people do today.

1 Timothy 6:10 NIV says that *the love of money is the root of all kinds of evil*. Would this verse make sense if the word *sex* replaced the word *money*? The love of sex has certainly proven to be the root of many evils. Think about that. What immoral acts can the desire for sex cause a person to commit? The list is long. Self-control and good judgment must be the rule.

- - - - -

The Bible is God's Holy Word. It contains the instructions for how we should live our lives. Our belief in God means we will trust His plan for our lives. To know the plan we must pray, read our Bible, and meditate on His word.

Proverbs 3:5-6 NIV states, **5Trust in the LORD with all your heart and lean not on your own understanding; 6in all your ways submit to him, and he will make your paths straight.** You may be one of those people who think the Bible is vague—that the Bible doesn't relate to the issues we face today. The Bible is like a textbook of life lessons. Sure the people in the Bible did not have cars and cell phones, but the problems they faced were not unlike ours today. God's willingness to intervene in their situations is the same as it is today. There are many different translations of the Bible and some are more easy-to-read than others. One that many people like is the New International Version (NIV). Read it when it is quiet and think about its words. Then pray and ask God to speak to you and reveal its meaning. Yes, the Bible does have specific information about sex. In fact, God created sex. He created it to be enjoyed in marriage.

Genesis 1: 27-28 NIV
Genesis 2:24-25 NIV
Genesis 3:6-7, 23 NIV

[27]So God created mankind in his own image, in the image of God he created them; male and female he created them. [28]God blessed them and said to them, "Be fruitful and increase in number.

[24]That is why a man leaves his father and mother and is united to his wife, and they become one flesh. [25]Adam and his wife were both naked, and they felt no shame.

[6]When the woman saw that the fruit of the tree was good for food and pleasing to the eye, and also desirable for gaining wisdom, she took some and ate it. She also gave some to her husband, who was with her, and he ate it. [7]Then the eyes of both of them were opened, and they realized they were naked; so they sewed fig leaves together and made coverings for themselves.

[23]So the LORD God banished him from the Garden of Eden to work the ground from which he had been taken.

You are probably familiar with the story of Adam and Eve. God created Adam, the first man on Earth, to watch over the Earth, take care of the animals, etc. in the Garden of Eden where he lived. Adam was told not to eat from the Tree of Knowledge of Good and Evil or he would die. From his side, God made a woman, Eve, to be Adam's wife and his helper. Eve was told by the serpent in the garden that she *could* eat from the Tree of Knowledge of Good and Evil, that if she did it would make her smart, as smart as God. She ate from the tree and shared the fruit with her husband. After this first sin, they became ashamed to be naked, and they were punished by God.

The book of Genesis is the first book of the Bible, and several aspects of sexuality are explained immediately. God understands sex and sexual desire because he created it— "male and female he created them." There are intentionally two genders, male and female so that we complement each other. Adam and Eve felt no shame about being naked because they were husband and wife. Their union, their marriage, was blessed by God, they had no restrictions from each other's bodies. They had no baggage, no sexual histories, no possibilities of STDs, they were both pure and wholesome creatures. Their time together in the garden was intended to be pleasure-filled. They were told to "be fruitful and multiply," which means that God wanted them to have sexual relations with each other resulting in children.

When the serpent or snake, spoke to Eve, he told her to ignore God's rules, to disobey God. The serpent told her to sin. He advised her to conduct herself as she pleased, to use her own mind, that God's plan should not be her consideration. The serpent convinced her that she did not need to control herself in terms of abstaining from the Tree of Knowledge of Good and Evil. Once she decided to exercise her free-will, she and Adam became aware that they were naked, and then they became embarrassed about it. This is why they covered themselves. As punishment for their sin, God caused many problems in their relationship, (Genesis 3:14-19) and sent them away from the paradise of the Garden of Eden.

Prior to sin, everything for Adam and Eve was perfect and lovely—it was as God intended it to be. They were a happily married couple. They were two naked, sexual beings living in a glorious place. Once there was sin, the splendor of their lives was disrupted. The Bible makes it clear that sexual relations should only take place between husband and wife. The Bible also makes it clear that sexual immorality is a sin. Sex outside of marriage is a sin that can cause a major disruption to the life God intends for you to have in your future. While casual sex may be a common occurrence among people you know and associate with, it does not have to be an activity in which you participate. It causes many problems. The big obvious problems are stress, potential STDs, and potential unwanted pregnancies, but there are underlying psychological problems that often we cannot pinpoint that stem from faulty sexual relationships. Not having a sexual history will make your marriage pure, healthy, and uninhibited—as God intends for it to be.

Think About It:

17-1 What are some of the problems that can be caused by the love of sex?

17-2 How can viewing pornography give you a sexual history that can cause problems in your marriage?

17-3 What are your thoughts as you read Proverbs 3:5-6?

17-4 What is your reaction to knowing that God created sex to be enjoyed in marriage?

Quote by John R. W. Scott from www.goodreads.com accessed June 12, 2016

**A person without self-control
is like a city with
broken-down walls.**

Proverbs 25:28 NLT

18 ~ Sexual Immorality

The Bible refers to any sexual relations outside the bounds of marriage as sexual immorality. There are many scriptures on this topic.

Proverbs 2:16-19 NLT
[16]Wisdom will save you from the immoral woman, from the seductive words of the promiscuous woman. [17] She has abandoned her husband and ignores the covenant she made before God. [18] Entering her house leads to death; it is the road to the grave. [19] The man who visits her is doomed. He will never reach the paths of life.
Wisdom is our deep, broad understanding of people, events, occurrences, etc. that we encounter. By having wisdom, which starts with the fear of God (Proverbs 1:7), we are protected from the temptation of many of our fleshly desires. Wisdom enables us to see situations clearly and turn away from those that will lead to our detriment. This book is intended to give you some wisdom. Of course you are free to ignore everything you have read, but it would be to your detriment to do so. Remember the chapter about pornography? These verses say that wisdom will save you

from the immoral woman, the seductive words of the promiscuous woman.   An immoral woman is one who frequently participates in sin, it goes on to indicate that it is sin of a sexual nature. She seduces men and has sex with many men (promiscuity). Pornographic videos are filled with these types of women.   Their intent is to seduce, and watching will lead to addiction, and a life that is far-removed from the life God intends for you to enjoy one day with your wife. Proverbs 4:5 says **Get wisdom, get understanding; do not forget my words or turn away from them.**

Proverbs 25:28 NIV
[28]**Like a city whose walls are broken through is a person who lacks self-control.**
Think of the visual here, a person who lacks self-control is like a city with no order. The lack of self-control leads to chaos. Think of the walls of a city as its boundaries, without boundaries, it's a free-for-all. This book is to equip you with information to help you rely on two things in making decisions about sex—good judgment and self-control. You must have predetermined limits for yourself so that you don't have to make decisions on the fly when you're caught up in the emotions of a situation.

1 Corinthians 6:18-20 NIV
[18]**Flee from sexual immorality. All other sins a man commits are outside his body, but he who sins sexually sins against his own body.** [19]**Do you not know that your body is a**

temple of the Holy Spirit, who is in you, whom you have received from God? You are not your own; [20]you were bought at a price. Therefore honor God with your body.

The Bible tells us to run away from morally-compromising sexual situations and not to participate in faulty sexual relations. The Bible advocates abstinence. It goes on to explain that the Jesus Christ lives within our hearts and thus is a part of our body, so to participate in casual sex directly dishonors God.

I Corinthians 7:1-2 NIV
[1]It is good for a man not to have sexual relations with a woman." [2]But since sexual immorality is occurring, each man should have sexual relations with his own wife, and each woman with her own husband.

These verses acknowledge our desire for sexual intimacy and advise how and when it is good. Sexual intercourse is to be reserved for marriage. A man should have sex with his wife, and a woman should have sex with her husband. Unmarried persons should be abstinent. Yes, God does want you to have sex, the verse says should—that's an encouraging word—He wants you to enjoy it, and He makes provisions for you to do so—when you are married. Rather than putting so much energy into trickery and deciding at what point in a relationship sex should occur, your energy would be better spent in prayer, asking God if your girlfriend is the woman He intends for you to marry. If the thought of your girlfriend (or the girl you're trying to get close to) becoming your wife is repulsive, the thought of having sex with her should also be repulsive.

1 Corinthians 10:13 NIV

[13]No temptation has overtaken you except what is common to mankind. And God is faithful; he will not let you be tempted beyond what you can bear. But when you are tempted, he will also provide a way out so that you can endure it.

This verse explains that temptation is everywhere, that no temptation is greater than our will to avoid and endure it. We can always look to God to help us out of situations we deem against His will. When you are out with your girlfriend and things start heating up and you're tempted to go all the way with her, it's okay, even in the face of blue balls, or embarrassment from your friends, it's not beyond your ability to change the course of the evening. You must employ your good judgment and self-control. When you are at home and a pornography ad pops up on your phone screen, it is a normal temptation. You have choices, you can ignore it or you can click on it. God is faithful. Ask Him to help you find something else to do that will occupy your mind.

Acts 3:19 NIV

Repent, then, and turn to God, so that your sins may be wiped out, that times of refreshing may come from the Lord.

This scripture does not relate to specifically to sexual matters, but to sin. Sin separates us from God. We are to live lives that are pleasing to God—this means we must follow God's plan. **In the beginning God created the heavens and the earth.** (Genesis 1:1 NIV) Since God is the One who created the earth and all things in it, we must trust His design as far as how things should work and the order in which events should happen. We should date then marry, then have sexual relations, then children. Doing things out of order causes distress. You probably know someone who has done things out of order and the distress it caused. Get wisdom. God knows that we are human, that we all sin at some point in time. Romans 3:23 NIV states, **All have sinned and fall short of the glory of God.** Fortunately, God forgives sin. He forgives our sin when we repent. To repent means we ask God for forgiveness with a sincere attitude of remorse. Then we must stop the sinful behavior.

Think back to the chapter about Secondary Virginity. You may not be a virgin, but after reading this book, you may have had a change of heart. If you desire to move forward without participating in sexual immortality, ask God to forgive you for your previous behaviors and attitude. Move forward with your life without participating in sexual immorality. It sounds easy, but temptation is real, you may be thinking. Yes, but do remember, 1 Corinthians 10:13. Temptation is a part of life. God will not let you be tempted beyond what you can bear.

Any questions? God does not approve of sexual acts between the unmarried. If you believe in Him, God will live in your heart, and therefore be a part of your body. Other sins, such as lying or stealing, are outside of the body, but sexual immorality is a sin against the body—the body in which the Spirit lives. Galatians 5:22-23 NIV states [22]**But the fruit of the Spirit is love, joy, peace, forbearance, kindness, goodness, faithfulness,** [23]**gentleness and self-control. Against such things there is no law.** Once a plant matures it gives forth fruit that contains seeds to be spread across the world. This passage about the fruit of the Spirit, in other words, says that once the Spirit of God is within us, we should carry ourselves with love, joy, peace, forbearance, kindness, goodness, faithfulness, gentleness and with self-control. There is no law against showing the world these traits, in fact, we are encouraged to display these characteristics in our behavior everyday.

The temptation to commit sin is always there, always! You cannot escape the temptation to sin. In our society, it is difficult to even escape sexual ideas—it's on TV, it's online, it's in your textbooks, your friends talk about it, people send you sexually explicit texts, pictures, girls walk around half-dressed, touching you, urging you on, it's everywhere! To overcome the images and pressure, you must have self-control. Self-control is the ability to deny yourself and control impulsive behaviors. The limits you set for yourself must be rigid and determined beforehand. It is nearly impossible to think clearly, make good decisions, and use self-control when another person is there and attempting to persuade you otherwise. Only you know what's good for you and the goals you have set for yourself. You are the only person who can make sound decisions about your conduct. That is, you and God, are the only ones capable of making these sound decisions. He has a plan for you and you must consult Him through prayer and through reading the Bible to know His plan for you.

"For I know the plans I have for you" declares the Lord, "plans to prosper you and not to harm you, plans to give you hope and a future."
Jeremiah 29:11 NIV

Think About It:

18-1 Had you head the story of Adam and Eve before? Did you interpret those verses in a similar manner as was explained here?

18-2 Do you agree that the love of sex can cause evil behavior?

18-3 Do you think the Bible is clear on its position on abstinence?

**Without the Sun
there is no shadow.
Without the Son
there is only shadow.**

Anthony Liccione

19 ~ Still Not Convinced?

All this talk of the Bible and sin and the Fruit of the Spirit may not be your thing, but please read on. You've read the previous pages of this book, there's just a little more. You haven't been brainwashed yet—see, a pretty girl just walked by and you just lost your place in the reading! Read on, you will not be brainwashed if you read these last few paragraphs.

You may not be a Christian. You may not believe in God. You may have never read or even held a Bible in your hands, but many people believe that God is the source of all wisdom, that He has the answer to any question we can pose. The Bible, the book of God's insight, contains the word LOVE as many as 800 times, depending on which translation you consult. For you, love may have never entered the equation in your past relationships, but I guarantee it's on the mind of the females you encounter. It's a common thing for young guys to use the word love to describe their feelings towards a particular girl, but the feeling may or may not be genuine. Love is difficult to define, but the Bible defines it in the following way: [4]**Love is patient, love is kind. It does not** envy, it does not boast, it is not proud. ⁵It is not rude, it is not self-seeking, it is not easily angered, it keeps no record of wrongs. ⁶Love does not delight in evil but rejoices with the truth. ⁷It always protects, always trusts, always hopes, always perseveres. (1 Corinthians 13:4-7 NIV) Not many people would describe love in that way. Very few people are able to live up to the standards set by this passage. As we, here on this earth, seek love from our many relationships, and we encounter people who will be special to us, we must never forget that the greatest love of all is God's love for His children.

Whether you know God or not, His love is there for you, and God loves you without any limitations. To make His love complete, you must learn to love Him in return and conduct yourself in a manner that is pleasing to Him. God's love is absolutely enduring, it is unchanging, and it is given to us by His grace. There is nothing that we must do, and nothing we *could* do to deserve God's love.

Many years ago, God sent His son Jesus Christ to live on Earth as a person among other peoples. Jesus endured many hardships and great cruelty, although he personally had done nothing wrong. His suffering represented the sinful world in which he lived. Jesus was later crucified (put to death) on the cross as punishment for the sins of the world. His death saved us from having to die for our own sins. Three days following Jesus's death he was brought back to life as proof of God's power. In the Bible in John the 3rd chapter (NIV), it states, ¹⁶"**For God so loved the world that he gave his one and only Son, that whoever believes in him shall not perish but have eternal life.**" God wants us to acknowledge Him, trust Him, and live according to His plan. When we do these things, He forgives us for our wrongdoing (sin) and promises that when we die, our soul will not perish, but we will live eternally, with Him in Heaven. In order to grow spiritually, we must pray, read our Bible, and tell others about His love.

God loves you. He wants you to believe in Him and trust that He will guide you throughout your life. If you have never accepted the love of Christ into your life, please pray this prayer.

> *God, I need you in my life. I need you to forgive my sins and help me to live a life that is dedicated to You. Lord, I believe that Your Son, Jesus Christ died on the cross for my benefit and right now I want You to come into my heart and make me the person You want me to be. God, I thank You for Jesus and I thank You for Your love and grace and mercy. Amen.*

If you prayed that prayer, (prayed it, with a sincere heart, you didn't just read it…) then you are now a Christian! A believer! You are saved! 2 Corinthians 5:17 NIV states **Therefore, if anyone is in Christ, the new creation has come: The old has gone, the new is here!** Your sins have been forgiven. You will have ever-lasting life with the Father in Heaven. You have a new story for your life. The next step for you is to find a Bible-based church to join that will support you and help you to grow in your faith. Through your faith in God and your prayers, God will give you the inner strength you need in order that you will always use good judgment and have self-control. These are the ingredients that will help you to be abstinent until you are married—just as He desires you to be.

Think About It:

19-1 So, have you been brainwashed by this book? What were your thoughts about the book—was it a learning experience?

19-2 Are you now convinced that sex should be saved for marriage?

19-3 Did you pray that prayer? If so, the author would love to know. Send an email from www.kimberlyga.com.

Quote by Anthony Liccione from www.goodreads.com accessed June 26, 2016

Scripture References in this Book

- 2 Samuel 11-12
- 1 Timothy 6:10 NIV
- Proverbs 3:5-6 NIV
- Genesis 1:27-28 NIV
- Genesis 2:24-25 NIV
- Genesis 3:6-7, 23 NIV
- Genesis 3:14-19
- Proverbs 2:16-19 NLT
- Proverbs 4:5 NIV
- Proverbs 1:7 NIV
- Proverbs 25:28 NIV
- 1 Corinthians 6:18-20 NIV
- 1 Corinthians 7:1-2 NIV
- 1 Corinthians 10:13 NIV
- Genesis 1:1 NIV
- Galatians 5:22-23 NIV
- 1 Corinthians 13:4-7 NIV
- John 3:16 NIV
- 2 Corinthians 5:17 NIV
- Romans 3:23 NIV
- Acts 3:19 NIV
- Proverbs 3:5-6 NIV
- Jeremiah 29:11 NIV

Holy Bible: New International Version. (2005). Grand Rapids, MI: Zondervan.

New Living Translation Study Bible. (2008). Carol Stream, IL: Tyndale House, Inc.

Q & A for the Author

Do you believe an abstinence-only
sex education is sufficient?

No, in the sex/health education programs offered by most US schools, there is mention of abstinence, but students are largely taught about various methods of birth control. I think these programs need more emphasis on abstinence. I realize that everyone will not accept the message of abstinence, so alternate methods of protection are necessary. I think abstinence should be explained and explored thoroughly before any other birth control methods are considered.

Why would you write an abstinence-only book?

I think it is important to empower teens with the emotional power of self-control. Many sex/health education programs use fear as the primary tool to promote abstinence. They show pictures of diseased sex organs, and emphasize the failure rate of various methods of birth control. This book emphasizes self-control as the best birth control, and gives teens the tools they need in order to develop self-control.

I am a Christian and the Bible promotes abstinence. I believe it would be irreverent to write a book that talked about abstinence, then offered other options (condoms, pills, etc.) to individual who are not married. To do so would promote sexual immorality. There are many scriptures that make it clear that God considers sex outside of marriage to be immoral. In society, however, the abstinence message gets lost in the idea that we only live once or that we're only young once. These ideas tend to set teens up for a lifetime of trouble. I wanted to write an abstinence book to help teens realize the value of self-control in saving their sexuality for marriage.

Since you're all for abstinence, would it be fair to say that you think sex is bad?

Absolutely not! Nothing could be further from the truth. I think there is an appropriate time and place for sex, and that is within marriage.

How is *A Guys' Guide to Abstinence* different from the *A Girls' Guide to Abstinence*?

I wrote the Guys' Guide after the Girls' Guide was nearly complete. I believe there exists a double-standard in what we teach our daughters and sons about sex. We say that girls should say no and boys should be careful. I must admit that, to an extent, I bought into that double-standard, which made writing A Guys' Guide to Abstinence very difficult. Then I kept asking myself, who would buy A Guys' Guide to Abstinence when most people don't even believe in abstinence for guys? Again, I had to realize that this double-standard is a human concept, the Bible does not differentiate its message.

I took a different approach in the Guys' Guide. Girls tend to be driven by feelings, while guys are more driven by facts. The girls' guide addresses how young women should manage their feelings in relationships, while the guys' guide deals more with probability, scientific data and the need for self-control. Both books are infused with short stories to help the reader put the informational chapters into perspective. Most of the informational chapters differ among the books, and the short stories are different, too.

KIMBERLY GIFFITH ANDERSON

I am a wife and mother who lives in South Carolina. My name is actually Kimberly Griffith Massey, but my published name is Kimberly Griffith Anderson. My heart grieved for 16 years as a high school science teacher as students constantly fell into trouble due to their sexual behaviors. This book will hopefully fill the gaps of what I have said to many students, and educate those I will never have the pleasure of meeting on the dangers of sex outside the bounds of marriage.

Yes, there is **A Girls' Guide to Abstinence**, too! Please spread the word about both of these books. I enjoy speaking to groups who have read my work. To contact me, visit my website at www.kimberlyga.com. Thank you for reading.

Other titles by
<u>Kimberly Griffith Anderson</u>
But I Love My Husband
(ISBN: 978-1-4969-1370-8)
But We're Not Married
(ISBN: 978-4969-7017-6)

Look for
A Girls' Guide to Abstinence,
(ISBN: 978-1530956586)
too!

www.kimberlyga.com

More by Kimberly Griffith Anderson

If you enjoyed the short stories in this book, you will really enjoy the author's novels!

These novels are about a teen couple whose romance results in an unexpected pregnancy. They experience lots of trials as they try to decide what to do. Eventually, he becomes a single father at age 19. You will enjoy these page turners. Order or download them from www.amazon.com or from www.kimberlyga.com.

Good Girl : ISBN 978-14384370938
Single Dad 19: ISBN 978-1438981949

**HUMAN
TERMS**

"I speak in human terms because of the weakness of your flesh.
For just as you presented your members as slaves of uncleanness,
and of lawlessness leading to more lawlessness, so now present
your members as slaves of righteousness for holiness."
Romans 6:19 NKJV

Thank you for reading.
Please post your comments at
www.kimberlyga.com

Made in the USA
Middletown, DE
29 June 2022

68073416R00086